The
Work
of the
Soul

Past Life Recall
& Spiritual Enlightenment

The

Work of the Soul

Past Life Recall & Spiritual Enlightenment

Edited by

Barbara Condron, D.M., B.J.

Essays by
Daniel R. Condron, D.M., M.S.
Pam Blosser, D.M., B.A.
Paul Blosser, B.A.

SOM Publishing
Windyville, Missouri 65783

© May, 1996
by the School of Metaphysics No. 100156
Portions of this book were previously published by the School
of Metaphysics in 1993 in the book
Total Recall: An Introduction to Past Life & Health Readings

Cover Art by Sharka Glet

ISBN: 0-944386-17-2

Library of Congress Catalogue Number pending

PRINTED ON RECYCLED PAPER
IN THE UNITED STATES OF AMERICA

If you desire to learn more about the research and
teachings in this book, write to School of Metaphysics,
National Headquarters, Windyville, Missouri 65783.
Or call 417-345-8411.

When it is viewed as an Eastern religious concept,
reincarnation is an idea far beyond the devotee's experience,
much like Christianity's Heaven and Hell.
In either you must wait until your life is over
to see how you did.

But when reincarnation is viewed as a scientific hypothesis,
it becomes integrated in today's thinking
and the distance between yesterday and tomorrow
dissipates in the light of understanding.

It becomes very clear that we are each here to do
the work of the soul.

It also becomes clear that the work of the soul
is the labour of love, given and received, throughout eternity.

—Dr. Barbara Condron

FOREWORD

by Dr. Barbara Condron

For some time now I have been contemplating the considerable range of ramifications the knowledge that *reincarnation is the means by which man's soul can mature* has upon my thinking.

Twenty years ago, I learned the difference between reincarnation and transmigration. This was an important first step because the idea of a mature soul returning as an animal or plant which generally-speaking are earlier and lower on the evolutionary ladder never made sense to me. That concept became the basis for an intellectual prejudice against reincarnation which supported the Christian bias I had been taught as a child. However, the idea that it might require more than one lifetime of experience to grow in wisdom, to gain perfection, to become Christ-like, was an idea I could reasonably consider.

My open-mindedness brought me into very good company, as I learned many great minds – from Cicero to William Butler Yeats, from Siddhartha Gautama to Richard Wagner – considered returning to the earthly schoolroom a part of man's spiritual development. Early in my research I came across this epitaph penned at the age of 22 by Benjamin Franklin, whose genius I greatly admire:

The Body of B. Franklin,
Printer,
Like the Cover of an Old Book,
Its Contents Torn Out
And
Stripped of its Lettering and Gilding,
Lies Here
Food for Worms,
But the Work shall not be Lost,
For it Will as He Believed
Appear Once More
In a New and more Elegant Edition
Revised and Corrected
by the Author.

Was this eloquently veiled reference to death and rebirth just the product of a young man's active imagination? Considering the wisdom of Franklin's consciousness and the varied activities of his life, I believed it was profound insight. It would seem so did he, for at the age of 79 he wrote, "When I see nothing annihilated and not a drop of water wasted, I cannot suspect the annihilation of souls, or believe that [God] will suffer the daily waste of millions of minds ready made that now exist, and put himself to the continual trouble of making new ones. Thus finding myself to exist in the world, I believe I shall, in some shape or other, always exist; and, with all the inconveniences human life is liable to, I shall not object to a new edition of mine, hoping, however that the errata of the last may be corrected."

Franklin's idea of rebirth, of incarnation, of the continuity of existence, was one I could understand and embrace. Removed from any particular religious dogma, be it Eastern or Western, I could approach a spiritual concept reasonably and from my own experience and perception. I too had witnessed God's creation. Without man's interference everything in nature is used to its fullest, expressing all of its energy. I had to agree with Voltaire when he concluded, that it is no more surprising that a man be born twice. Everything in life is resurrection. It made sense that God must have a higher purpose for man than living only one physical life and then spending an eternity in rich reward or desolate punishment. Although I did not yet grasp what that purpose might be, I knew I possessed a strong, reasoning mind and I believed I was given that mind to use, not to squander.

The acceptance of individual responsibility for learning and soul progression has had broad influence in my life. I found I could answer the "why?" questions of life; they were no longer over my head, left only to the mind of God. Everything in life – from the newborn who will eventually be a king to the person who is fired from his job, from the babe born with birth defects to the person whose life is spared while many others are killed – has a cause that can be identified and a purpose, a reason, to exist. Possessing this awareness is a large part of the reason why I dedicate my life in service to the progression of humanity.

Early in my metaphysical studies and disciplines, in fact at about the same age that Franklin was when he wrote his epitaph, I moved from accepting the *possibility* of reincarnation to *knowing* that reincarnation is the means by which the soul of mankind matures toward compatibility with his Creator. Learning how to access and read what is called the Akashic Record erased whatever doubt remained in my thinking. The Record is a universal memory of the thoughts and actions of people, places, and situations. Individual physical memory is stored in the brain; this universal memory is housed in the soul. Physical memory is employed by the waking conscious mind while universal memory is exercised by the inner subconscious mind.

Using spiritual disciplines I learned at the School of Metaphysics, I began to strengthen my recall skills. Drawing upon subconscious mind I could perceive what had occurred in the distant past, as you might recall present-day childhood experiences, and then trace the influence and impact of that past to current experiences. In this way, the reality of reincarnation and karmic indentures began to affect the way I think and the way I act.

This knowledge of reincarnation has made me more responsible for the quality of my thinking, particularly the intention I hold for my actions. I now have more than sympathy or pity to offer someone who is less endowed than myself. I now value the indomitable spirit and will of every person to learn, to grow, to mature. I also realized I have experienced in many times, in many places on the earth, in many physical forms. Although most of my incarnations have been in female form, I have also experienced as male. I have been Caucasoid, Mongoloid, and Negroid and combinations of the three. I have been rich and I have been poor, master and slave. I have been Buddhist, Hindu, Zorastrian, Christian. It is this awareness that lets me see life from my soul's perspective. It helps my consciousness to transcend the limits of the physical body because I realize its impermanence. This awareness frees my consciousness to be devoted to what exists beyond the physical – the spirit that is the Real Self. And it enables me to perceive and align my thinking with the work of the soul.

American automobile mogul Henry Ford adopted the theory of reincarnation at the age of 26. He said, "Work is futile if we cannot utilize the experience we collect in one life in the next. When I discovered Reincarnation it was as if I had found a universal Plan. I realized that there was a chance to work out my ideas. Time was no longer limited."

I too began to realize a different nature of time. Some who have a superficial acquaintance with reincarnation believe it an excuse for all forms of irresponsibility the least of which is procrastination; the wasting of time. I have found the opposite to be true. Reincarnation strengthens self-reliance, self-discipline, self-control, for you and no one else are responsible for your intentions in your association with others. There are no victims. There are no scapegoats. There are no special deals. The laws that govern our universe, such as the Law of Karma, are just and exact. They will be fulfilled. They cannot be cheated or twisted to meet a particular person's need.

The seeds you sow bear the fruit that you will harvest. If there is not time to reap the harvest in the present lifetime, there will be time in the future. The good you think and do, the understandings you glean, the wisdom you achieve become a permanent part of your soul. This is the true work of the soul. Accessing the Akashic Record reveals the nature of the work you are here to accomplish. Drawing upon this memory you begin to see through the eyes of your soul and thus you become familiar with the work your soul must do. Some call this work karmic indenture, and so it is. Becoming aware of your karmic obligations frees you to meet them. As long as you are ignorant of the work you are spiritually blind.

The Past Life Readings that are offered through the School of Metaphysics reveal the specific karmic indentures impacting your life now. They give valuable spiritual information that is not readily available. As a worldwide community we have yet to evolve sufficiently so that children are taught to use their full potential and thus glean information from past lives themselves. It is increasingly true that many children do remember past life experiences. It is also true that their talk of "when I was the daddy.." or "where I used to live..." is more often met with parental indifference, amusement, or even disdain than with investigative interest that leads to verification. This is the common state even though the information is available to everyone, at all times, at all places.

There are those whose questions demand answers. Their experiences, fleeting though they may be, serve as a spiritual thorn spurring them to seek answers and deeper understanding. Some, in their curiosity and yearning to find answers, seek the clairvoyant who can see what they cannot. If they are fortunate in their choice, the seer is wise and advanced in spiritual development having the capacity for intuitive insight and the common sense to give truth while respecting the person's right to choose. However, as in every profession there are charlatans and imposters. There are the ego-driven who mix what truth is perceived with what they think you want to hear because it will feed their coffers. Or the psychological professional who seeks human guinea pigs under the guise of past life regression therapy. As with anything in life, it is rewarding to be informed.

School of Metaphysics' readings are an outgrowth of the research and study of mankind's potential spanning a quarter of a century. These readings have been given for thousands of people on six continents. They are provided by teams of two who have received specific education and training in using subconscious mind to access information from the Akashic Records. The reader and conductor willingly volunteer their time and skill to aid others, for each of them see this activity as serving our fellow man. They do not accept personal financial reimbursement for their time and effort. Chances are you have not met the reader and conductor, at least not in this lifetime. You do not have to be present for the information to be gained for you.

What you will receive from the reading is an image of you, your loves and hates, your desires and fears, your talents and shortcomings. You will better know yourself. You will have a greater understanding of why you do what you do and why the people and situations exist in your life as they do. You will know your karmic obligations and have keener insight into your purpose for life. You will indeed become aware of the work your soul is here to do.

The Work of the Soul introduces you to three types of significant Past Life Readings. You will meet many people, from all walks of life, who share the questions you have asked yourself: *"Where did I come from?"*, *"Why am I here?"*, and *"Who am I?"* People have found the readings to be candid, genuine, and revelatory to their everyday lives.

*"Of all things which a man has,
next to the gods, his soul is the most divine
and most truly his own."*

— Plato, *Laws*, 4th century B.C.

*"The soul is the master of every kind of fortune:
itself acts in both ways,
being the cause of its own happiness and misery."*

— Seneca, *Epistolae*, 63 A.D.

"No soul shall bear the burden of another." — *Koran*, c. 265

*"The soul is the primary principle of our nourishment,
sensation, movement, and understanding."*

— St. Thomas Aquinas, *Summa Theologiae*, 1272

*"Each of us possesses a soul, but we do not prize our souls
as creatures made in God's image deserve,
and so we do not understand the great secrets
which they contain."*

— St. Teresa of Avila, *The Interior Caste*, 1577

Table of Contents

Part II
Crossing of Paths Readings

Part III
Family Readings

(I) do nothing but go about persuading you all,

old and young alike, not to take thought

for your persons or your properties, but first and chiefly

to care about the greatest improvement of the soul.

I tell you that virtue does not come from money,

but that from virtue comes money and every other good of man,

public as well as private.

— Socrates, *Plato's Apology*, 4th century B.C.

Introduction

The Work of the Soul Spans an Eternity

by Dr. Daniel R. Condron

The School of Metaphysics offers a comprehensive course of study in applied metaphysics. The course is designed to develop the student's awareness and understanding of the three divisions of mind and inner levels of consciousness. At the time I completed the study I didn't see any other place to use my time more productively, both in aiding myself and others, than in my capacity within this organization, the School of Metaphysics. I now spend most of my time teaching and serving in administrative capacities at the international headquarters of the school in Windyville, Missouri, where we receive correspondence and serve people from all over the world each week.

All my life I had attempted to be productive in my pursuits. First it began in physical matters, whether basketball or student body president or Dean's list in college or graduate school. But all those things, after a while, failed to satisfy. With any of the five senses, you can only enjoy so much cake. You can only see so much light until it hurts your eyes. You look at the same landscape and it's beautiful for a while, but if you had to look at it twenty-four hours a day you'd want to see something else. The smell of a rose or even pepper is appealing, but too much of it and you're tired of it or it hurts. Even the desire to touch something or feel something can wane. Grabbing a baseball bat can be fun and enjoyable but if you hold any muscle too long it will begin to atrophy.

All of our senses have the capability to give us pleasure, but when they are overused or when you take them to the maximum after a while they fail to satisfy.

If it hasn't already come for you, there will come a time when you've reached the point of appreciating the joy you have in your life, the experiences and whatever satisfaction you've gained through your life, but there is still a desire for something that seems missing. That something is the real Self, the inner Self. It's the you. Where does that real Self exist? It exists in the inner *mind.* When most people hear the term mind they think of a physical brain but this is not what I mean by mind. The brain is like a computer. It is an organ of the body as are the heart, the liver, and the lungs. If the brain is an organ similar in function to a computer, what drives it, what directs it? The conscious mind gives the brain commands much like a computer programmer directs a computer's function. What then directs the conscious mind? We can go deeper and deeper into man's existence, to the subconscious levels of mind and the superconscious levels of mind, eventually reaching the point of "I" sometimes called in Eastern literature, the real Self. In the Bible or other Holy Works you may hear it referred to as "I Am". It is the *Self,* the identity and the individuality that is you.

If you've never tried this experiment before, sometime try it. Stop your thoughts and discover what goes on when there is no thought. Find out where you are when there is no thought. Find out what your existence is when there is no thought. If you haven't yet disciplined your mind enough to enter that stage of no thought, then practice it this way, look to see what happens between the thoughts. Look to see who you are or what exists between your thoughts. This is a good experiment and you'll make some productive discoveries. If you desire more control you will pursue a concentration exercise every day, whether you are holding your full attention on a candle, your fingertip, or a dot on the wall. Any stationary object can be the subject of a concentration exercise. In fact, that is how a mantra or a chant, a particular vibration such as Om that you say over and over again, has the same type of effect. The difference with an external object like a candle flame is you are using the sense of sight as the point of focus so your mind can remain still. With the chant or repeated vibration, the sense of hearing is the focal point for the attention.

What do the senses, the attention, the identity and this individuality have to do with reincarnation or past lives? To reincarn, to move from one body, release it, and move into another, you must be doing something in the times between using a physical body. Who is that *you* existing between physical bodies? Where does the Self exist all the time you are in a physical body during a lifetime? Where is the *you* who exists between lifetimes? These are ways to consider the Real You and seek ways to find the Real You.

Reincarnation is similar to the experience of dreaming. You have your waking day's experience, then you go to sleep at night. Where do *you* go? Where does the conscious mind go when you sleep? Perhaps you believe it shuts down. Then, who is in your dream if it is not your conscious mind? When you awake the next morning, perhaps you discount the memory of a dream experience as being meaningless and you get ready to go about your daily physical routine. If you didn't need that dream time, if it wasn't a process of assimilation and preparing for the next day's experience, then all you would do at night would be to lie down and rest your body. Then after one hour or ten hours depending on how hard you worked your body that day, you would be up and ready to go again. You would never need sleep. But there is a need for sleeping time. There is a need for time to harmonize, to process, to integrate, what has been experienced with the waking mind into the inner mind so the two can work together.

Reincarnation is similar because in a sense a whole lifetime is relative to a day in your life. One day is like a mini-incarnation in the sense that you come out into the physical for a day's experiencing then at night you move your attention into the subconscious mind where you assimilate the previous day's learning. At the end of a lifetime, you move your attention into the subconscious mind where again you assimilate the learning gleaned from experiencing. Since a day is twenty-four hours, sixteen or eighteen of which you are awake, it does not take long to assimilate waking experiences, perhaps five, six, eight hours. It takes much less time to assimilate one day's learning than a full lifetime's. As a part of reincarnation, assimilation is the process of coordinating and unifying the connections of experiences during the most recent lifetime with experiences from previous lifetimes. Assimilation is understanding how these experiences relate. A dream works in the same way. You have experiences today and they need to be coordinated with every experience you have had previous to this time.

Why? What would it be like if you went through grade school and then in seventh grade you studied some subjects that were totally unrelated to anything you had studied before? You would have no point of reference. Schooling is designed with the intention of adding to the material you've already learned. It is the same with a lifetime. You have the opportunity at the end of each lifetime to process the material and learning you've gained and add it to the subconscious mind's storehouse of permanent memory so you can prepare for the next lifetime just as you prepare for the next grade in school.

Some learn a great deal in a lifetime, others less. A lesson can be refused for a whole lifetime. This is similar to grade levels in school. If a student does not learn the material available, then he needs to repeat the opportunity to learn until it is accomplished. Learning is the individual's choice. Why would anyone refuse to learn a lesson? It doesn't seem to make sense, does it? One reason is they do not know how to cause learning. So many times you will hear people say, "why did this happen to me" or "I don't understand why my life's like it is".

As a Conductor of readings in the School of Metaphysics, I have had the opportunity to meet and serve people from all walks of life and of all nationalities. Many of the questions they ask in Past Life or Health Readings reflect a desire to understand. They want to know why something occurred in their lives or why other experiences tend to recur. In research and study, we have found the point of origin to be some kind of thought process. But most people don't remember their thoughts. They don't remember their thoughts from five or ten minutes ago, let alone yesterday, a week ago, a year ago, or ten years ago. If you consider thought as cause then the physical events in our lives, whether they be our health, job, or personal relationships with friends and family, are a reflection of those thoughts. Memory then becomes very important. If you don't remember your thoughts, how are you going to connect the causal thought with the physical outcome in your life when it arises a week later, six months later, or years later? Usually it doesn't take years for thoughts to manifest, however, if you keep the same thoughts the same situations will continue to occur.

It is vitally important for us to know ourselves. Knowing ourselves begins with remembering and identifying what our thoughts are. Not every single thought needs to be recognized, but rather the repetitive thoughts, the imagined limitations we create in our minds, the habits and compulsions, the way we restrict ourselves, and the way we react to similar situations. Our most beneficial characteristics are also important. We determine what a beneficial characteristic is by the greater fulfillment it produces in our lives, and the good and kindness we do for others. We can call this learning and growth, we can call it greater awareness, we can call it enlightenment, and these characteristics will always add fulfillment to our lives. When there is something missing in life it is time to learn a method to add what is missing.

Each lifetime, the Real You embarks upon a new journey with an express desire, plan, and ideal of gaining an understanding or permanent learning that will contribute to your soul's progression. This ideal is very specific to and for the individual. For one person, the desire may be developing a greater understanding of love; not just the love from a mother to a daughter, a husband to a wife, but an expansion of awareness to include the highest mental and spiritual expressions of love. This is the desire to understand love completely. For another, the ideal might be courage. The courage to stand up to the town bully, or the courage to fight in a war, or the courage to speak before a group of people. There are many expressions of bravery and it can be experienced and understood on every level of consciousness. What is important is knowing what your ideal for this lifetime is, what you most need to build within Self and what steps will build that understanding.

Love, determination, courage, value, authority, dignity, respect, and pride, are some of the qualities that we need to develop in order to become whole. Some of them we have already built. Each of us has our own unique set of permanent learning that we've earned. To different degrees each of us is using part of that learning. Maybe you've taken a course in college. You stayed up all night and studied before finals and you got an A in the course. Six months later you don't remember anything you read. You've also passed courses of understandings in past lives. This produced permanent learning that has become a part of permanent memory stored in your soul. You are probably not bringing forth and using all of your understandings this lifetime. By developing total recall you can access what is stored in your personal subconscious storehouse.

One of the interpretations of the word *educate* is "to draw forth". This is exactly what happens when there is true learning. When you push yourself beyond previously accepted limitations you can achieve anything you desire. Some people have limitations of age, "I'm too old" or "I'm too young". Others think "I'm the wrong race", "wrong sex", "my hair color's wrong", "I was born in the wrong country", "I was raised in the wrong environment", "I don't have the right education". We can spend our whole life thinking of excuses for why our lives fail to bring fulfillment. What is really important to determine in life is what you want and what you need. This is where trust enters. Trust of your inner voice, for some hear it as an inner voice. For others it is trusting what seems right, a feeling deep in your solar plexus. For others it is following what they know to be the right thing to do.

Sometimes these interests and desires go back to childhood. Sometimes we don't discover a place or a way to use these truths until later in adult life. We find all along we've been preparing to use a lifetime. Anyone who has decided to follow the path of Self development and awareness, one who has chosen the route that will cause the quickest soul evolution and makes that the number one priority in life, will be the one who progresses the fastest. You can focus all of your attention on one physical object, another person, or anything in this wide, beautiful world. If you focus enough attention over time you will achieve what you desire. When you're really honest with yourself and willing to learn from the efforts you make, you will achieve it. The same is true of soul evolution. When you give soul progression your full attention and full energy, then your return will be in that area.

A lifetime is a very short thing when you think about it. I didn't think that fifteen years ago, but one year is only 365 days. You've got 70, 80, 90, or 120 of those years. Make the highest use of the time you have. The degrees I earned from the University of Missouri are in agricultural economics. In economics, one studies benefits and costs. I like to talk about choices and events in terms of the highest return. What is the greatest investment you can make? The investment is *you*, this lifetime. *You* and your 70, 80, or 90 allotted years in this physical body you've chosen. That is your investment. The highest return you can achieve on your investment is a return that will be permanent. Physically we look for permanent or semi-permanent investment such as property. We can put money in the bank or buy stocks and bonds and spread out investments. Many people invest in these areas expecting a return. When you buy a piece of property it is not going to disappear off the face of the earth, it will be there for as long as you own it. Anything you build on that property can last a long time when it is given maintenance and upkeep. Spiritually, the greatest investment is permanent learning, for this is how we invest in the soul. Permanent learning exists beyond the lifetime, indeed forever. The investment in the Self is the greatest investment because it gives the greatest return.

Many people, both contemporary and historical, have believed in reincarnation. Almost three-quarters of the people living today believe in ideas of reincarnation, but all that kind of information can be readily found in your local library. I accepted the idea of reincarnation because it made sense to me from the first time I heard it while attending college. The part that originally made sense to me was the idea that I am more than a physical body. If I am important and my life has meaning then it must continue having meaning after 70 or more years because this is not a wasteful universe. Man can be wasteful but the universe uses energy completely.

Many people have had psychic experiences. Before I began seriously studying metaphysics, I had psychic experiences that taught me I was not the body. I was sleeping in bed one night and I felt a great vibration which preceded a golden ball of light coming from my chest. The next thing I knew I was up on the ceiling looking down upon my physical body. That was proof for me. You can read about similar experiences such as those who have experienced near-death experiences, or patients under anesthesia on the operating table who watch doctors perform surgery on their bodies and later relate what the doctors were saying when they were believed to be asleep. These kinds of experiences are fairly common where people experience the self as separate from the physical body. For years I have practiced dream interpretation, recording my dreams almost nightly. After a while you begin to realize that in itself is an extrasensory experience. While dreaming you experience a place that is not physical and you are experiencing without use of a physical body. You experience and prove your existence apart from the body every night.

For almost thirty years, the School of Metaphysics has provided over one hundred-thousand readings, many on past lives, for people all over the world. These readings are thrilling because they aid each person receiving the reading to have an instantaneous awareness of who they are like they've never had before. Imagine that you have amnesia. You cannot remember anything that happened before yesterday. You would be functionally impaired. There would be many things you'd be unable to do that you take for granted now. See how limited you would be? Imagine, when you can have the information of who you were before this lifetime, how much more it offers you. A past life reading reveals information about the you you were before this lifetime.

What's the difference between you now and you in the 1700's or 1300's or 2500 B.C.? Two things: one, experience, and two, the degree to which you have used those experiences. If you chose to use your experiences for progression you are significantly different. You have probably many times watched two people experience the same situation. One gets mad, the other one breaks out in laughter. Each reacts according to their unique experiences, and the difference shows in how experiences have been used to build security in the Self. For the one who lacks security, a situation will arise threatening the security, and the person will feel the need to protect the self becoming angry. For the confident person, an opportunity will arise and inner security will provide an objectivity enabling them to keep the situation in perspective and even find humor in it. Each lifetime we have the opportunity to create learning for ourselves. We also have the right to choose how much learning we will create. You don't have to wait five lifetimes to reach the level of awareness you desire. You can quicken your soul growth or spiritual development. It's important to trust yourself.

Past Life Readings are like evolutionary vitamins. Today we take vitamins when food fails to provide the value the body needs. A Past Life Reading gives you instantly something your mind can use that it needs. The conscious mind and physical body did not know how to find the answers that the past lifetime offers you immediately. The first time I received a Past Life Reading I knew I'd received in ten minutes more knowledge about me than I had gained in the entire preceding year. It wasn't magic. It was no more magic than you turning on the television and watching a report on what happened in China or Russia or Brazil or Canada. Yet, a hundred years ago you'd probably be doing pretty well to hear of world events at all unless you happened to be a sailor who traveled around the globe. Television provides an increase in the efficiency of communication. An idea or image originates at one point on the globe and can move almost instantaneously to you, the receiver, located at another point on the globe. This is exactly what Past Life Readings do. They retrieve or collect information from one place that you do not have access to normally, and present it to you. The great thing about the reading is that all the information is about *you*! That really is the most valuable information there is.

I love history because history tells me where we have been. It tells me where we came from. Perhaps you think, "History's not about me, I'm here right now." It was *you* existing in a different physical body and living what we now see as history. The more you can know about your Self the better. The first key to change is Self knowledge. When I say change I mean it in a positive sense. Many view change negatively. A hurricane hits the coast of Florida, killing hundreds and destroying thousands of homes. That's change, change is bad. However, change does not mean destroying something, rather change is creation. When new houses are being built, that's change. Change is accepting what is in your environment, creating something better, and in the process bettering you.

Each one of you is vitally important. You are vitally important because you are a soul, a spark from the Creator. You are vitally important because you are *I AM*. You are also vitally important because every step up the soul ladder of evolution you make places you in a much greater position to aid others. You never know when one kind word offered from your value and wisdom may go all the way around the world and come back again. You can affect that many people beneficially, that's how important you are. If you've not accepted it to this point, it is time to accept your importance. To accomplish something greater than what you are, to accomplish something beyond what you have created already, requires something that is always available and that is imagination. Unfortunately, not enough people practice using it, but fortunately more and more people are beginning to use imagination. You can call it visualization or creative mind, but it is the image-maker, the ability of the mind to form images. For you to create anything with intention, it is required that you first have a mental image. If you were to go from where you are to Cairo and you had no mental image, no map, you could go north or south or east or west and you wouldn't know how far to go. Without a mental image you wouldn't even know if you had passed it already. It would take you forever to get there! With a mental image, or in this case a map, someone giving you directions, or memory of having been to Cairo before, you can go directly where you desire.

A Past Life Reading serves as part of that mental image road map because it gives you a snapshot of one section of who you are. This kind of reading gives the past lifetime that is most significant to the present – one of your past lives out of all the many that is relative to you right now. What makes that lifetime significant is not a "what" but *who*. You make it significant by your particular set of situations and circumstances and most importantly the attitudes that you hold. For instance, the most important thought you hold in mind can be positive or negative. It can be love or hate, will power or passivity, these are just extremes of a quality you were attempting to develop in a past lifetime and left incomplete. You started to pursue that quality, did some activity toward and gained some learning of it, but you did not complete that area of your learning. Now this lifetime you are fortunate. You have created situations and opportunities to complete that area of your learning. The Past Life Reading will reveal what was left unfulfilled in a previous life and give significant insights for fulfillment in your present life.

Look at your life. You will see that anytime you had a goal that matched your desire, you first had an idea born from your desire to experience something. You earned your ideal through action, putting forth the effort necessary by making changes in your Self. And you were fulfilled. In fact, you were not only fulfilled when you achieved the goal, but you were gaining joy and enthusiasm for living life all along the way because it was your special goal and sacred desire. You knew it was what you wanted to do. You can share that awareness with people all through your life because it has value and benefit.

It is very satisfying for me to be able to offer the readings to people. To see the look of realization on a person's face, to recognize the joy at finding an answer to a question that has been bothering someone a long time, or to see the fulfillment of learning something about Self, that's worth more than any amount of money. It is about the happiest feeling and experience anyone can have. Maybe you know of someone who has saved another's life. Maybe you have had this experience yourself. You can imagine or remember the joy experienced from this noble act. The Past Life Reading offers insight and truth to the person requesting it which can contribute to a greater life than he or she has now.

There is nothing more important than realizing *who* you are. It is important that you decide the quickest, fastest way to achieve that Self awareness and Self knowledge and pursue it. By opening the doors of permanent memory you begin your journey toward total recall and give yourself the wealth of what you have already attained. Command of memory spurs the imagination to *become* and evolution is quickened. What you add to yourself will last for an eternity.

Part I

Past Life Readings

*"It is no more surprising
to be born twice than once,
everything in nature is resurrection."*

—*Voltaire (1700's)*

What sets Man apart from all other expressions of Creation on this planet is the ability to reason. This developed thinking capacity has caused Homo sapiens to search for answers to questions that can only be conceived by an inquisitive, creative mind. *"Where did I come from?"*, *"Why am I here?"*, and *"Who am I?"* For thousands of years, many have become content to meekly accept the beliefs of someone in a position of authority. Upon receiving answers to some of their questions, other queries remain unasked by a mind that agrees to only follow the leader. In this way, Man's inherent urge to create and evolve is stifled, his mind entrapped in physical identity and his thoughts the victim of imagined limitation. However in every generation, in every culture, there are those who dare to challenge limitation. They are the true pioneers amongst us.

The world, this physical school room for the soul, has become a much smaller place in the past century. Modern technology has given us the means to have immediate access to what is occurring in every corner of the planet. From a politically motivated assassination attempt to motion picture awards, from a medical advancement in conquering disease to Olympic sports events, if it holds import for humanity the events are publicized almost as quickly as they occur thus becoming common knowledge.

Yet too often it seems our ability to disseminate information is unequal to our ability to assimilate it. Thus what could be a source of greater contentment, peace, and security becomes a stimulus for greater confusion, fear, and misunderstanding. We are finding that knowledge of the world around us does not automatically bring the growth in awareness which will produce the kind of world we want for ourselves and our children.

For instance, researchers estimate the average person in the United States will have three or four careers during his lifetime and reports show most are not equipped to effectively handle these changes in life. It is becoming common knowledge that we tend to repeat patterns throughout our lives, for instance the spouse we choose tends to have more relevance to our same-sex parent than we probably originally intended. Scientists continue to find no reason for the aging of the physical body, yet it does indeed occur. No matter how many physical actions and reactions someone else identifies, the information received can only be of true benefit when it is understood and put to use in our own lives. Our imagination must move beyond the confines of what is familiar, what is comfortable, what is physically recognized as real.

Imagine. How would your life change if you knew the purpose for your existence? How would this knowledge affect your choices in life, your relationships with others, your general attitude toward living?

How would your consciousness change if you could remember your existence *before* the birth of your physical body in this lifetime? Would it alter your awareness of the meaning of physical life and open doors to new knowledge of the continuity of Self as spirit? Could it answer the many questions physical life leaves unanswered?

How would your attitude change if you knew your manner of thinking is the governing power determining the quality of your mental, emotional, and physical health? Would freedom from fear of illness encourage you to think, and therefore act, more productively and positively?

Throughout history there have always existed those individuals who identify with what exists beyond the physical. They exercise the mind's thinking abilities far beyond the norm. These people have dedicated their lives to answering these universal questions. Self reliant, they are not too proud to embrace the thinking and experience of others that might accelerate their own quest toward enlightenment.

You have heard of these people before. They are history's heroes and heroines. They are the philosophers who mastered the law of relativity. They are the scientists who mastered the law of cause and effect. They are the inventors and artists who mastered the laws of creation. They are the kings and queens who mastered the laws of divine birthright. They are the Spiritual leaders who mastered the law of existence. Each of these is an individual like you and me. Individuals possessing the same universal structure of mind and functioning within the same Universal Laws that we do today. Each of these individuals displayed the enlightenment of an advanced soul.

The inquiring mind wonders what separates history's heroes and heroines from the average, normal, and common man. The answer is found through study, application, and understanding of the nature and purpose for our existence. The faculty and students, both past and present, of the School of Metaphysics respect individual intelligence and creativity, recognizing that the destiny of all human beings is heightened Self awareness. For this reason, the mission of the School of Metaphysics is to promote peace, understanding, and good will within Self and among all people by aiding any individual to become a Spiritually Enlightened being. The heart of SOM research is the nature and structure of mankind's consciousness – spiritual, mental, emotional, and physical – a means for the advanced soul to accelerate his or her spiritual development. What has been discovered about human potential goes far beyond what is currently accepted about mind-body relations.

This research dares to enter the domain, up to this time, ruled by religious dogma. Our research transcends diversity, elevating awareness to the point where religion and science unite in understanding. Thus the soul becomes more than a philosophical concept. Rather the soul is a part of every individual; a deeper essence of Self that exists before the present physical self and will exist past the time of the present physical self. The soul is the part of yourself revealed in your dreams. When the "unexplainable" happens – telepathy, clairvoyance, miraculous healing – the soul is often at work.

Our research proves the soul is accessible to the concentrated waking mind that has become disciplined and skilled in spiritual practices. Our course of study is a series of universal principles combined with mental and spiritual disciplines intended to expand your consciousness toward spiritual enlightenment. The many educational services that have come from our research are designed to fulfill our purpose of ushering in Spiritual, Intuitive Man. The service which probably has personally touched the most people is the reading consultations.

Thousands of people on six continents have received some type of reading from the School of Metaphysics over the past quarter century. Those desiring optimum health or who are experiencing health difficulties find the Health Analyses helpful. This type of reading reveals the mental, emotional, and physical disorders that are eroding wholeness, many times uncovering what others have not found and always offering suggestions that will promote healing and health. Health is the greatest of all gifts that we can give ourselves, for where there is health there is quality in the life. For this reason, the information revealed during a

Health Analysis is priceless.

Intuitive information can also aid in our professional lives. The Business Analyses examine an entire company as a vehicle possessing a mission and guided by an intelligent director(s). Business Analyses are similar to the Health Analyses for an individual for they provide what statistical research cannot. Business Analyses tell the owner what weaknesses exist in the company and give suggestions for investing your time, energy, and money to accomplish your company's objectives. In terms of the savings gained – whether from identifying faulty wiring or embezzlement, production mistakes or employee apathy – by knowing your problem areas and the profits made from when suggestions are implemented, these analyses go far beyond any research designed to aid the employer that is currently available.

The third type of reading, and the subject of this book, is the Past Life Reading. A Past Life Reading introduces you to your soul in a way you have probably not known before. It reveals a part of the journey your soul has made to reach your present life circumstances and state of awareness. These readings describe a past life that your soul has experienced: who you were, what you were doing, where and when you lived, what your loves, desires, fears, and doubts were. Most importantly this is not just any lifetime that is related, rather it is the *most significant lifetime to your present lifetime.* This is the most unique and most valuable part of these readings. The information is relevant, and therefore immediately helpful in understanding the conditions and situations in your *present* life.

For many, the Past Life Reading introduces them to their soul. It gives you a glimpse of life from your soul's perspective by revealing the karmic bonds that keep your soul earthbound. And it offers suggestions for releasing those bonds. You begin releasing your engrossment in the limits of your physical self and begin to identify with the Real You, your soul. As the import of connections and repercussions of your past life to the present sink into your consciousness, you find yourself answering the why's of your own life. At last you are aware of your purpose, your mission in life. You are finally free to do the work of your soul.

Past Life Readings
by Pam Blosser, D.M., B.A.

Questions from an Open Mind

Where do I come from? Why am I here? Where am I going? These age-old questions are the link to the deepest yearnings in Man. There is an order to the universe and the surrounding world. There is purpose to life and an order to its seemingly disjointed string of events. Why? Why? The urge to understand and know Truth propels the reasoner to search for answers extensively both inwardly and outwardly.

I, too, have asked the question why. While living in London and taking a year-long intensive course in the Maria Montessori Method of Education I asked myself this question. While I was there, I met a young street poet named Peter. Peter had a collection of folk instruments among which was a beautifully handcrafted folk harp called a clarsech. I enjoyed spending time at Peter's flat working on assignments for my education course. We both enjoyed the freedom of going about our own business knowing that there was someone close by but without feeling obligated to entertain each other or getting distracted from our own goals.

One evening I was at Peter's apartment working on my projects. Now Peter was an avid soccer fan and this particular evening he announced he would be going down the street to watch a soccer game. I told him I would like to study in his living room while he was gone. I usually studied in a small room off the living room, but thought I would enjoy the change of scenery since the rest of the apartment would be empty. He said fine and in a short time was out the door.

The living room was where Peter kept his folk instruments. It was distracting to sit in the room with them, especially the beautiful harp. It rested in a dark corner of the room quiet yet alive with music ringing within its dark wooden frame. I looked up periodically at the harp as I worked, my attention moving back and forth from my notebook to the harp in the corner. It silently beckoned me to its side to touch its dark, wooden frame and stroke its silken strings.

Finally I laid my papers aside and approached the beautiful instrument. Sitting down behind it I pulled its wooden frame back against my right shoulder and lightly plucked its strings. How wonderful! Each touch was music! The progression of sounds made a tune and the accompanying strings wove a harmony around the melody line. As I played, my only thought was to discover how many tunes I could create. I looked up at the clock and to my surprise forty-five minutes had passed. I could hardly wait for Peter to return.

When he walked in the door I excitedly related to him what I had experienced. "I have to have a harp to take back to the States with me!" I exclaimed.

Within a few days Peter had located a harp maker who lived on the south side of London, the other side of London from where I lived. Together we went to his shop where I purchased a harp to take back to the United States. I loved my harp immediately as if it were a long lost friend. It seemed so delicate and vulnerable as I carried it back all the way across London. I had to transfer several times on the subways and buses to make the connections. How weary I was as we arrived at Peter's flat.

I wondered how I was going to get my harp back to the States. I would just have to take it on the plane as carry-on luggage. When I got to the airport I was told the harp was too big and I would have to check it as luggage. I worried about the harp all the way across the Atlantic Ocean like a mother worrying about her child on her first day of school.

When I was settled back home, I began to compose and arrange music on my harp. I did this by ear – something I had never done before. The music I created was unique, in a category by itself. My music was haunting, sometimes lush. The chord progressions I chose seemed almost other worldly.

At that time I knew little about past lives but I asked, "Why?" Why was there a strange and comfortable familiarity with this instrument? Why did it seem so easy to arrange and compose music on it? Why was it that the music that came so easily seemed so different from any other music I had heard before?

Answers from Unexpected Places

Shortly after I returned to the United States I took a job teaching in a Montessori School. I also came across a brochure about the School of Metaphysics. I was looking for spiritual discipline. The brochure outlined such areas as concentration, meditation, healing, the power of the mind and Past Life Readings from the Akashic level. Much of what I read made sense but the Past Life Readings left me cold.

First of all, reincarnation was something that I hadn't seriously considered and I had never heard of the Akashic level before. I called and talked to the director of the school, asking her several questions about the classes and services offered by the school. One of these questions was about the Akashic Records.

She explained to me that the Akashic Records was a "place" within the inner levels of mind where everything that had ever been thought, said, or done in the physical world was recorded. To me, it was like a twilight zone between the spiritual and physical realms and this was where the information for Past Life Readings was stored. Anyone knowing the right steps could tap into and draw out the information much like keying into a computer and requesting information to come forward. It all sounded pretty far out to me and I told her so.

She invited me to an open discussion coming up a few nights later and I decided to go. The topic was on psychic happenings, another area that seemed far out to me. What impressed me that evening were the people at the center – down-to-earth, straightforward, practical minded and most of all, relaxed. When I left that night I felt more peaceful than I had felt for a long time. I wanted to learn how to have that sense of peace too. I immediately enrolled in the classes, beginning the spiritual discipline that would aid me in building the peace of mind I wanted to attain.

The classes revolved around practical skills of the mind so very little was mentioned about reincarnation, Past Life Readings, or the Akashic Records until it came time for my class reading after Lesson Eight. A student at this point in the lessons has developed a certain amount of understanding through the mental exercises and can respond to the information in the reading making productive changes. One afternoon, Brad, a teacher at the school, approached me about my class reading. Lamely I muttered, "I don't think I'm ready for it."

Brad laughed and exclaimed, "Now I've heard everything." With that remark I knew I was going to get my reading whether I wanted it or not, no matter what kind of excuse I could find. I had come to know that the teachers at the school would support me in my strengths but definitely not in my fears.   I was resigned to the idea but reassured myself that I didn't have to believe in reincarnation as a result.

The day of my class reading arrived. I was met by my teacher, Merala Heins, as I entered the school. We chatted for a few moments in the kitchen and then a rather large man with a goatee sauntered into the room. My teacher introduced him as Dr. Jerry Rothermel, president of the School of Metaphysics. He announced that it wouldn't be long before we would be starting.

I walked into the living room.   Seated on the couch was a delicate looking young woman, her blonde hair pulled back in a bun at the nape of her neck. She had settled in the middle of the couch, her hands relaxed in her lap, her eyes closed. Dr. Rothermel seated himself to her left. After speaking to her softly for a few minutes he said: *"You will search for the identity of the entity referred to as Pamela Elizabeth Stewart. You will relate a significant incarnation for this entity."*

The Reader began speaking.

> *"This one is seen as female form. We see this to have been in an area now known as England. We see that this one had accepted a position at a very young age as that of governess and that this one would be taking care of another's children. We see that this one began to use much of this one's creativity and imagination, and began to establish many of the educational outlets for these children. We see that this was very impressive to the parents of the children, as well as to the others who saw the results of this. We see that there were contacts made in which this one was allowed a great amount of education but most of this was in a teaching capacity. We see that eventually this one was very much involved with the higher education of this time period. We see that this one dealt with many subjects for every day there was a need to create an interest in a particular subject which this one would use. We see that this was due to the creativity and the enthusiasm with which this one taught. We see also that*

*there was a great ability which this one developed in relating
what was in the knowledge to that of the physical life of the
students, which made the subjects much more real and the
students much more interested in the studies."*

I had never met this Reader before. Yet she could "see"
attributes about me that made so much sense and fit so well. In the
present lifetime, I had taught a variety of subjects from cooking to
swimming to English as a second language. Teaching had always come
easily for me no matter what the subject. There was no way she could
have known about me. I had not mentioned to my teacher or anyone at
the school the many subjects I had taught during my life. Following the
description of the past lifetime, the Reader offered how this information
was significant to my life at this time.

> *"In the present time period there is a great need in regards
> to the many abilities which this one has. We see that there
> has not been a connection made within this one's life at the
> present time to see the abilities and to see them in action and
> the results which they will incur. We see that there is a great
> creativity which this one applies quite accurately to the
> physical. We see however that this understanding has not
> been brought to this one's attention and there has been an
> attitude established upon this one's part that self is starting
> from the very beginning. Would suggest to this one however
> that there is much knowledge to be drawn on of a practical
> nature as well as of an abstract nature in this one's previous
> understanding. Would suggest to this one that the purpose
> of the present time period for this one is not just to take
> information or to take from the situations on how to learn or
> how to apply the teaching concepts but there is much that this
> one has to give also and it is time, in order for this one to
> fulfill this purpose, to put this into activity. This is all." (9-
> 29-77-1-CK)*

The reading fit so well with my new job at the Montessori
school. In spite of all the experience I had had in my life, teaching at the
Montessori school seemed brand new. It seemed I had much to learn.
What if I had actually been this teacher? If so, I knew more about
teaching than I was giving myself credit for. I could stop being so

nervous about not knowing enough and trust my intuition about teaching.

After hearing the reading it was no longer important to argue about reincarnation as a fact. Arguing about the existence of reincarnation seemed like an intellectual mind game much like arguing about how many angels could dance on the head of a pin. It seemed trivial in comparison to the importance of using each day of life. What I learned from that reading in regards to reincarnation was the importance of time.

Each day – even each moment – is like a reincarnation. This moment is affected by how you've used the ones previous to it. How you use the present moment will have its effect on the ones to come. What you do with each moment of your life is important. You choose whether you're going to learn and change or do the same thing you've always done. With the first choice there is growth; with the second, limitation and stagnation.

Within your daily activities if you make a mistake you have the opportunity to correct it. If you're practicing a sport or a song on the piano you can practice it again until you become proficient at it. Your imagination is your resource to improve the quality of these attributes. If you don't like what you did yesterday you can do something different today. If you did like what you did yesterday you can do it again today and possibly reach a greater depth of understanding with it. Each day you can find out just how strong or courageous or tolerant or patient or persistent you have become. These individual choices determine how full of learning and growth your life is. And isn't this what life is all about? You are here to learn who you are as a creator, what kind of creator you are and what kind of creator you can be.

The more I explored reincarnation as a day-to-day physical progression of learning, the more sense it made to me to apply this principle to its spiritual level. Each lifetime, as you learn through your physical experiences, you, as a soul, can add to your identity of who you are as a creator. You can discover just what you're made of as you face and respond to life. You can identify the height of integrity to which you are reaching, and you can admit as you experience what you create what kind of mental creator you are.

Assignments from the Soul

Just like you have the memory in your brain of the yesterdays leading to today, you also have a sense of the continuity of the steps in your learning from lifetime to lifetime. This is stored in the permanent memory of your soul called the subconscious mind. Most of you, however, are not consciously aware of the steps you have taken as a soul that have brought you where you are now in your own evolution. Most of you have forgotten how to access the information in the Akashic Record – the holder of your soul's past. Nor do you remember how to access your own subconscious mind – the holder of your understandings. These understandings are qualities such as courage, compassion, self-value and a sense of order, to name a few, that you have built through repeated purposeful action in previous lifetimes. They are now a permanent part of your identity.

You might think of your mind as a giant iceberg. Only the top of the iceberg appears above the surface of the water. This is the part of yourself that you can experience with your five senses. It is called your conscious mind, your physical body, and to some extent your emotions. Now look below the surface of the water and what do you see? The majority of the iceberg exists below the water's surface just as the majority of yourself exists "below" the surface of your own conscious existence. This vastness is your soul, your spirit, your essence. If you identify with the physical body only it would be like thinking that the tip of the iceberg is all of you that exists. What is real is only what the iceberg can see, feel, hear, taste, and smell. You as the tip of the iceberg identifies as incomplete and separate. The quest to understand who you are is to identify with the whole and reunite the iceberg once again.

Each lifetime you have the opportunity to explore a chosen facet of yourself to be united with it, or to make it part of your identity. In the beginning of evolution this completeness was more like a blueprint of your potential than the finished product. It takes the soul and the physical conscious identity working together to identify each part of the blueprint and then actualize it.

The actualization process begins with a belief – a belief that you are strong or organized in your thinking, for example. It is a belief in yourself that you can create something valuable in your life. By applying this belief in your daily life you have an experience that calls for the quality you believe you have. You discover just how strong or organized you really are. Then it becomes a knowing. You know through the experience that you are as strong, stronger or not as strong as you believed you were. If you believe you can be stronger you begin to imagine what you would do differently the next time a similar experience occurs in your life. This reasoning process gives you a place to grow and expand your identity toward your real potential. Each time you respond to a belief that you are valuable to humanity you are setting up a condition to learn something about yourself and unfold your identity – fulfill the blueprint, as it were. Evolution is this process of unfolding.

The soul needs the physical self in this process because knowing comes only through purposeful experience. These experiences do not "happen haphazardly". They are caused intentionally by yourself out of a need to identify and understand. Now this Self I am referring to is not the self that can be tasted, touched, seen, heard, or smelled. I'm not talking about the tip of the iceberg. I'm talking about your soul. Your soul knows what parts of the blueprint have been fulfilled and what parts are yet to be fulfilled. Your soul perceives the physical experiences as the means to fulfill this blueprint. Your soul draws you, the outer self, "mysteriously" to these places of learning. And your soul receives the understanding from the experience into itself as a permanent part of your identity. The outer self feeds the soul by learning from experiences.

Each lifetime it is the soul that chooses what physical conditions will offer the best opportunities to begin the learning process for that lifetime. Then it is up to the outer self to cooperate with this learning process by the choices it makes. How well are you living up to the learning your soul or inner Self has assigned to your physical or outer self? As the following excerpt reveals, fulfilling the soul's assignment is the key to happiness in our present life.

> *"We see at present time within this one there is a love that this one does have for structure and discipline. We see at those times when this one is devoting the mind and devoting the Self to some form of discipline that this one is very content, for this one does reach greater understandings and does produce what this one desires in her life. We see*

however there are times when this one does scatter the attention and does not pursue what is true to this one's desires and at those times when this one is turning away from what this one truly desires, this one does become very unhappy." (7-26-90-10-LJF)

When information concerning past lives is made known, you can enhance your ability to define who you are by adding to what has already been built within the Self. Notice how in the following reading examples there was a quality gained in a past life now being added to in this lifetime. The first is of a female who in a past life was raised in a poor family in the Middle East. There was much love in this family. She was taught as she grew up that she was beautiful, she had much love and she would always find blessings in whatever experiences were in her life. She perceived her hard work as a labor of love and a giving to God. She knew she would be rewarded in the afterlife. She was seen by others in her community as a source of freshness and joy and she passed these ideals on to her children. In that lifetime she learned about loving and giving unconditionally.

In this lifetime she is adding to this understanding because she is discovering that although she wants to give, there are those who do not want to receive from her. She is learning she need not gauge the value of her love by how others wish to receive. Rather her lesson is to continue to give freely, respecting those who do not wish to receive and seeking out those who are receptive to her love.

The second example comes from a reading of a female who lived a past life in Italy in the 1500's. In this past life she used music as a way to draw her family together during times of hardship and conflict. She took a deep responsibility for the harmony in the family and in so doing became personally involved with their lives. She developed a great knack for listening and offering counsel to others.

In this lifetime she possesses a concern for other people and uses the listening and counseling skills developed in that lifetime. She is learning to relate what she gives to others to her own growth.

"Would suggest that to cause there to be growth and aware-ness in the Self is to cause there to be an elevation of this one's availability and this one's service that can be given to other people." (9-28-90-1-BGO)

These are two good examples of how we can add to both our learning and identity from one lifetime to the next.

Reading the Records

A Past Life Reading is a valuable resource of information. In the School of Metaphysics, as part of the course work in the advanced series, students are given the keys to going into the subconscious mind at will, tapping into the Akashic Record and drawing forth desired information about their own past lives or the past lives of others. This information is also made available to anyone who desires it through the service of a Past Life Reading given by a trained Reader and Conductor.

The past life brought forth in a Past Life Reading is one significant to the needs of the person requesting it. The reading reveals information about a past life that relates to the present conditions and circumstances of that individual. This type of reading addresses the question: what thoughts are affecting current conditions in relation to the process of learning and soul growth. Was there a quality developed such as courage or compassion that could be drawn on now or developed further? A female who was a healer in China in the 1200's is now being told to evaluate the abilities and talents from previous lifetimes so she can offer them to others. Another female who learned about self-control, self-discipline, maintaining a sense of peace and calm, and of identifying her own source of being in her lifetime in China in 500 A.D., is now being told to use that self-control and self-discipline in order to learn to focus on the quality of serenity.

Was there learning avoided in a past life that now is being faced again? A Past Life Reading offers much more than a means to satisfy curiosity or inflate the ego. It serves to stimulate the ego to act from the perspective of the information revealed.

In a past life, a female was born into a family in Italy in the 1700's. Her brothers and sisters were quite a bit older so she was raised like an only child. During that lifetime she was very creative in the fields of singing, dance, drawing and painting. She spent much time alone pursuing these interests and isolating herself from others. In this lifetime she once again deals with a sense of isolation in her need to associate with others. It was suggested that:

"In order for this one to understand and to love this one's own self and to create the identity that this one wants this will involve association with others for it is in association with others that this one does truly understand what this one has to give and what causes this one to be unique." (7-25-90-9-LJF)

Because the Past Life Readings relate to the present situations in a person's life it relates to the karma of the individual. Karma is a Sanskrit word meaning "to do" or action. Karma relates to the cause and effect action of the universe. This means any action will produce certain results. The action referred to here is not just physical action but more significantly mental action or intention. To illustrate, here are two situations. In the first, Joe is gagging on some food and John wants to save him. He administers the Heimlich maneuver to dislodge the food in his throat. In the second situation John is angry at Joe and wants to hurt him. He comes up behind him and grabs him in the middle to knock the breath out of him. The physical action is the same but the mental action is different. In the first situation John wants to help Joe; in the second, he wants to hurt him. The mental action or intention is what causes the karma and it is relieved through understanding.

Karma is an educative process. It is one of the best methods you have of gauging where you are in your spiritual growth. Here is an example of how karma works in a physical sense. Let's say you are going to bake a cake and you know how much flour, sugar, eggs, baking powder, and vanilla to add but you don't know how much salt to add. You add the salt you think will work. When you eat the cake you find it needs more salt. You have just experienced karma because you have experienced the results of what you caused. You recognize the amount of salt is out of balance with the other ingredients. The next time you make a cake you have the opportunity to correct the amount of salt. When you have learned the right amount of salt to add to the cake, by again experiencing what you cause, you have relieved your karma. The amount of salt is in proportion or in balance with the other ingredients in the cake and you can reproduce a delicious cake every time.

Here is an example of karma in a reading where the individual is learning about being true to inner desires. The individual, a female in this lifetime, was a male in New England. Her name in that lifetime was Benjamin Edward Montague. As a young boy he experienced love and concern from his parents which gave him a sense of security. However, his parents sent him away to a boarding school because it offered him a greater education than the school in the area where he lived. The teachers within this school emphasized discipline but without a sense of love or concern. Benjamin had difficulty learning under these conditions. He counted the days when the school year would end so he could return home.

His parents would not listen to his desires to change schools and Benjamin was afraid to be too insistent or to voice his desires. Benjamin responded to this condition by establishing the attitude of life being hard and having to fight to enjoy or really use a situation. On top of this Benjamin became a lawyer, a profession he cared very little about. He would much rather have been a doctor or veterinarian. He did well at his profession even though he found the work boring and did not care to be around the criminal element.

> *"We see that this one built understandings of consistency and follow through on just about whatever he decided to do. We see that this one did also build an understanding of love in this one's family but this did not extend to the rest of the life."*

The karma that was left unfulfilled dealt with learning the difference between unselfishness in giving and sacrifice.

> *"We see in the present time that this one has difficulty making choices in the life direction that are based around this one's own fulfillment or the meeting of this one's needs. We see that this one makes choices where this one puts the self in very difficult situations and does not know why other than this one thinks this is what this one should do. We see that there is a need to recognize that when the greatest love does occur within this one is when this one makes the choices in this one's life based upon this one's desires and fulfilling those desires. It is important for this one to learn the difference between this one fulfilling this one's desires and falling into a rut of selfishness that causes stagnation, for distinguishing this is important for this one's development of*

this one's own trust and to really live the life fully and as
respectfully as this one needs to do." (6-16-90-3-CSR)

What this individual realized from the reading was to pursue desires, to trust the inner authority and feel comfortable with it. To fulfill the inner desires, serving other people is necessary so that both the Self and others benefit. This was the "missing link" in understanding that could now be applied. Real change or understanding comes through experience and practice.

Paying Karmic Debts

Although karmic experiences most often involve other people the karmic debt is always to yourself. Remember it is the intention behind the action that actually sets up the karma. That intention is yours and no one else's. No one "does anything to you". They do stimulate and influence you, but you have the free will to respond to their influence in whatever manner you choose. In one reading it was suggested that:

"When this one does experience reactions to others in this one's environment that this one identify what ways of thinking or acting are stimulating this one's anger or other reactions. For we do see that these others are mirrors for this one of qualities that are out of balance within this one's own Self. Would suggest from this point that this one then determine how this one would want to cause these to change." (1-16-91-8-LJF)

It is through coming to terms with your attitude and changing your response, until it is comfortable, to one producing growth that you are able to pay off this debt. When asked about karma with other people in a reading, the Reader replied:

"Would suggest to this one that in terms of this one's indebtedness, that this is in regards to her own growth and development. The response to the roles that other people play are according to this one's choices and that of others in terms of accelerating or retarding this one's growth and progression." (9-9-90-3-BGO)

Through your own choices you can actually speed up or slow down your soul growth. The best way to speed up soul growth is in giving. The best way to slow down soul growth is in holding back from giving. Here is an example of how an individual's dream was dashed in a former life and how he holds back from giving this lifetime. The reading revealed that in the previous life the man had been an architect in England. He had a dream to build a decorative and powerful sculpture to be placed at the gate of his city and provide inspiration to those who passed. So precious and valuable was this dream that he was overly hesitant to communicate it to others for fear of being ridiculed. Yet this dream continued to be a driving force within him.

Eventually he met a wealthy man to whom he revealed his secret dream. This man supported him so much that he became his benefactor and agreed to front the cost of the building of this structure. The architect drew up the plans for the statue. Builders were sought out and contracted. But even as beautiful as the structure was and with the full support and respect of the benefactor, the builders thought it was a waste of time, money, and resources. Their opposition stopped the construction from taking place. The man's fear of his most precious dream being rejected had in fact come to pass. He was so disappointed he felt he had no reason to continue living. As a result his liver began to degenerate and after a time he died of a liver disease.

From this past life, the karma that still needs to be brought into balance or understood is the sense of vulnerability that ideas or dreams can be invalidated by what other people think or say.

"We see within this one there are great dreams and ideals that this one holds within the self and these give this one much drive and enthusiasm in this one's daily life. We see once again for this one to be very closed in this one's communication for this one is always afraid someone will take away from this one's self what this one does think and what this one holds dear to the Self. Would suggest to this one for this one to be very visionary, very clear and very brilliant in the expression of this one's thoughts. We do see this one to have much ability to be charismatic. Would suggest for this one to bring these visions closer to home by incorporating the idea that the individuals that are in this one's life at the present period of time are those who are

*compatible with this one's desires. Would suggest to this one
to cease protecting the Self from others but to welcome them
into this one's mind, into this one's heart." (5-17-90-7-LJF)*

Karma will continue to exist as long as this man holds to the idea that others will take from him, as long as his intention is to protect rather than seek earnestly those who will receive what he has to give. Those not wishing to receive do not invalidate what he offers. Believing in his dreams and finding those who will receive will be this individual's first step in relieving his karma.

A reaction or non-productive attitude has its source in the inner Self needing to understand a particular quality or a truth. It is the way of thinking that is repeated from lifetime to lifetime until it is changed that produces the karma. When the attitude is changed it indicates the individual has matured to a new level of understanding. When one woman asked about her abandonment by her family during this lifetime and how it related to the past, the Reader responded:

*"These are attitudes that this one has created concerning
this one's own worth in relationship to other individuals.
Would suggest to this one it is not situations and circumstances
in the past that have caused the present attitudes; it is this
one's desire for understanding that produced this one's
creating the attitudes that this one does hold." (1-16-91-12-
LJF)*

There have been readings done when the most significant lifetime was of a well-known and historically recorded individual. Even in these readings there is karma to be brought into balance. A female in New Orleans received a reading when she had been a famous musician in Europe, however, the name of the musician was not forthcoming. Perhaps knowing the name would have distracted this person from the present-day learning available. Another woman in Columbia, Missouri received a Past Life Reading when she had been the famed explorer Marco Polo. Throughout the present lifetime she had travelled extensively throughout the world, much like Marco Polo had done in his day. The significance for her was to follow through on what she had started and complete the things left undone in her life. In another instance a male in Norman, Oklahoma had been an English philosopher,

Thomas Reid, in a past life. This lifetime was recent enough that he could find a listing in the encyclopedia. As he researched this historical figure, he was amazed by the corresponding information in the reading and in written history.

Deja Vu

As I continued building mental discipline in metaphysics classes, the idea of karma and reincarnation from the standpoint of soul growth made more and more sense to me. It made sense that we would have more than one lifetime to complete all the learning and realize the potential of the Whole Self. It also made sense that each type of physical condition in life, whether living affluently or in poverty, in a healthy body or a disabled one and so on, would offer some type of learning for the soul.

I also began to get answers to some of the questions I had asked myself concerning my harp. It made sense that a fascination or familiarity with a particular time period or country was a good indication there had been a lifetime there.

One of my students received a Past Life Reading when he had been a Greek warrior. Even though he had not fully accepted reincarnation, he had always held a fascination with Greece especially of the time period of his reading. This fascination was the beginning of the verification of reincarnation for him in his own mind. A special talent or knack, like a craft or an art, is an indication that it has been done before in another lifetime and a certain amount of proficiency has been developed. An artist in the present time learned from a Past Life Reading she had a great skill in creating art and different kinds of pottery in India in the 1700's. A student going to chiropractic school learned she had been a healer in China in the 1200's.

Also in developing my intuition and associating with those of like mind in the School of Metaphysics, my peers and I would often have "glimpses" of past lives. When I was playing my harp, one of my friends had a past life memory of my playing my harp in Greece. I had remembered a past life in early Greece when I had been a courtesan and had entertained many people with my music and dance.

Another friend related a past life memory of our being in a

temple in Egypt. I asked her about it because I also had a memory of a past life when I lived at the Temple Beautiful and worked with musical tones and their effects on people and objects. She described a large, white, airy room, partitioned and decorated with soft gauze-like cloth that rippled and swayed in the wind of the open air. The gauze-like partitions diffused the sunlight outside. What she described fit the memory I had of the temple exactly! Music and dance were a large part of my study and research at the temple. The music I produced at that time had a haunting, other worldly quality, much like the quality of music I now produced with my harp.

Another one of my classmates received a Past Life Reading when she had been a Canadian Indian in northwestern Ontario in the eleventh century. Years before she had joined the classes, she had actually left her comfortable suburban life as a housewife and moved to northwestern Ontario to homestead. She lived out in the wilderness fifty miles from the nearest town and sixteen miles from the nearest road. She had no electricity, no running water, no flush toilets, no radio or T.V. But as rugged as her existence was she adapted easily, even feeling comfortable and at home. She didn't know why she felt so comfortable until years later when she received the Past Life Reading.

Each of us is unique. The identity we have built through the understandings gained is our process of discovering who we are as mental creators. We have proceeded according to our own choices. The soul has chosen to incarn into a certain physical condition in order to add an understanding to the Whole Self. The soul uses race, sex, nationality, physical features, parents and country as a means of stimulating this kind of learning. Being born into a pleasant situation is no more a reward than being born into an unpleasant situation a punishment for something done in the past. Both are offerings of something to learn. In fact, the learning from a challenging situation is often apparent because of the qualities utilized to respond with a sense of dignity. In either case it is how you use the life's situations that cause the growth.

What could be learned by being born into a wealthy family or a poor family? In one situation a female was born into a wealthy family in China to offer her a place to progress spiritually.

"We see this one actually believed that this one's own self-sacrifice and this one's own self-discipline would benefit

*and cause those around the self to evolve. We see that this
one actually believed that in this one's own self-discipline,
it would cause the commoners around the self to evolve. And
this was done for them, rather than for this one's own self-
gratification. We see that the understandings built in that
lifetime were primarily of self-control, self-discipline, of
maintaining a sense of peace and calm, and of identifying
this one's own source of being." (6-16-90-4-CSR)*

By the same token, a male was born into a family of nobility in
France and dealt with a sense of value within himself. He ran away from
the opportunity to use his situation and learn about value and thus did
not add any growth to his soul.

*"We see this one to be raised with the idea that this one was
eventually to take over the position that this one's father had
and we see this to be a position with the government. We see
this one personally to think that this one was not capable of
living up to the grandness and the reputation and the kind of
honor that this one's family had. We see for this one to spend
a period of time in hiding where this one did travel and did
hide this one's identity and did pretend to be a peasant where
this one did not have to live up to the types of expectations
that this one had had." (7-25-90-10-LJF)*

Upon entering a new physical lifetime, the soul can choose the
physical form that will accelerate learning. For instance, the soul will
choose to be born into a male body for the opportunity to learn how to
be aggressive. Being born into a female body gives the soul the
opportunity to learn how to be receptive.

*"We see this one to be utilizing the male form at that time to
cultivate a certain type of aggressive expression. We see this
one to be very conscious of this desire to do so." (6-22-79-
1-SMB)*

A young woman asked why she had chosen to incarn in a female
body this lifetime. The answer was very enlightening to her:

"There is a desire on this one's part to understand the

process of creation. We see this one has practiced initiating action but that in regards to the commitment of the completing and receiving what has been initiated, there is learning that this one desires. [Regarding] this quality of understanding, this one made this choice." (1-16-91-9-LJF)

Being born into a particular country or a particular race affords the soul unique conditions in which to respond. One individual asked why he had been born in Iran. The answer revealed a particular quality that this country offered him, one that would stimulate him to bring out understandings of a poetic nature in the early part of his life.

"We see for this to primarily revolve around a love of beauty and the recognition of the beauty in thought and the recognition of the beauty in poetry, the recognition of poetry in life and the ability to view life as a poem or as a rhythmic movement. We see that this type of beauty is recognized only when there is the disciplining of attention and the disciplining of the ability to visualize not only outer things but inner things and how the inner things connect through their outer manifestations providing a link between the inner rhythm of what produces life and outer movement." (6-16-90-7-CSR)

A female asked why she had been born in England in this lifetime and why she had been adopted. The answer included the need for particular astrological influences as well as early cultural training for her learning. The reading went on to say the birth condition did not matter, the parentage did not matter, as long as she had the conditions for building independence and self-reliance. This is an example of how the soul will choose the best conditions to learn the lessons that are most important. In this case the physical parents were immaterial as long as the opportunity for learning existed.

Another female asked why she had chosen to be born in the United States this lifetime. The Reader related that this country offered freedoms and therefore the opportunity for her to choose. The soul in choosing certain physical situations sets up a mental condition for learning. The soul makes these choices in regards to the growth of the Self.

In a past lifetime in France, I was born into a body that was deformed. A portion of the right arm was missing and the pelvic area had not been developed, making it difficult to stand erect or walk. My soul chose to be born into this physical condition for a particular reason. I asked about this reason in my reading. The reply was:

> *"....to consider that to deal with and confront the situations that occurred as a result of this selection was a great opportunity to find strength within the Self."* (10-78-1-GAD)

When the soul chooses a difficult situation for the physical being, it offers an opportunity to build such qualities as strength or courage within the Self. How else will the individual know these qualities unless he faces a situation where he can exhibit and use them?

Possibility Thinking

This Past Life Reading offered a universe, as it seemed, of facets about myself – areas to build, develop and cause to mature.   In that particular past life, my family learned to accept my deformity but the community didn't. Early in life I had developed an image of myself as deficient and ugly. I also had great intuitive abilities and often had visions adding to the isolation and fear of myself and my family from the community.

My religious devotion was important to me. I would sometimes envision spirits of a religious nature that were highly revered. On two occasions during mass the congregation witnessed the presence of a light around me. Because the community was superstitious they reacted to me as a combination of demon and saint. It was not until the priests in the church announced that this translucence was from a spiritual source that I became accepted by the community. I even experienced some notoriety at this time as people desired counseling. During that time I took my attention away from my inner development and onto the popularity I was experiencing. I depended heavily upon attention and approval from outside influences for my sense of individuality and security. So much so that when the attention from the community had receded I experienced a sense of instability and confusion. I died shortly thereafter from a respiratory problem. The significance to that lifetime is as follows.

"We see in the present lifetime this one has carried through and is dealing, in a conscious and unconscious fashion, with many of the attitudes which were part of her innate self during that previous time period. We see this one to have the image within herself and to have had this since early childhood of extreme plainness and unacceptability through her expression in the physical sense. We see this one has attempted and has utilized many ways to compensate for this feeling. We see this one so far has not successfully released herself from this visual image of herself. We see this one also to again have the tendency to place and identify the self through reactions and external situations. We see this one to depend to a great degree upon external situations as a measurement of her own place and her own individual self. We see this one to deal often with an inner sense of isolation which has no basis in fact, or is not produced in actuality by the situations and the conditions of the life. We see this one to suffer from this sense of isolation and to have difficulty breaking through the wall and the barrier which it presents to herself. Would suggest to this one to recognize that the conditions of the physical existence are those which have been brought to the self as aids and supplements, that these cannot and should not be relied solely upon as a measurement of success or existence. Would suggest to this one to recognize that there is and will continue to be an innate, sustaining movement of existence and progression which is not eliminated nor obliterated completely at any given time. Therefore this one need not be concerned to sustain that externally nor to create it or to initiate it for it is already initiated, but rather to observe it, to know it and to complement it with that which is in the physical situation." (10-78-1-GAD)

It was as though the Reader had reached inside and touched the deepest parts of my Self. She had touched the part of me that lives within four glass walls and watches the world going by outside – the me that wishes to reach through that wall and give, fulfilling the deep desire to share and be a part of someone else's life. And in the giving I would not have to fear rejection or loss.

She had touched the part of me that tries to establish a sense of Self according to what others think. In truth, I had ended up losing myself in the process rather than building any image of my Self.

She had touched the part of me that reaches to be close to the creative, motivating force of the Universe, our Mental Father. The Reader had captured what could be within my Self with either its fullness and richness or its loneliness and emptiness.

There were so many parallels between that lifetime and this lifetime. I had experienced so often a sense of plainness and unacceptability. I had done many things to compensate for that feeling. As a child and a teenager I had strived to make good grades and be "the perfect girl" for my parents. I had made sure I was well-groomed and presentable to others. I had been active in my church and school through various clubs and organizations, scholastic and social. Yet inside I considered myself not good enough, always second best.

I had been afraid of being a bother to others so I would sacrifice my own needs to avoid what I considered might take away from someone else's needs.

And then there was the strong parallel to know my God and to be close to my Maker. As a child I had wondered about the magnitude of God's love, if he cared about every hair on my head! During my life I had searched for the spiritual through my religious upbringing in my church, through the practice of Zen Buddhism in Japan and now through the study and discipline of the spirit in the School of Metaphysics. It had been a motivating force and focal point in my life.

From this reading I began to believe I was beautiful. Somewhere I had been missing that part by adopting an image of myself as plain and unacceptable. I didn't have to work so hard at being acceptable. I already was. All that was needed was to discover and embrace it.

I had begun to see how I could build an image of being beautiful and acceptable as a young adult. How I wanted to be beautiful! But I wasn't. I thought of women who had beautiful faces but were not beautiful. I thought of women who were considered plain looking but who radiated a beauty that went beyond the physical appearance.

"If this is so," I thought, "then that means if I cultivate the inner beauty I can actually become more beautiful the older I get!" I began to imagine what it would be like to bring out inner beauty. It was a delight to imagine that I could possibly cause myself to become beautiful.

This Past Life Reading was bringing out a possibility – the possibility of causing a change in my way of thinking that could bring about a change in my Self and my life. By getting a chance to look inside I felt closer to my Self and more integrated with the parts that were inside – the parts that were lonely and the parts that were beautiful.

By responding to the information and suggestions in the reading, I was removing misconceptions about my Self as unacceptable and isolated, learning that other people wanted to be close to me just as much as I wanted to be close to them. I made a point of speaking to people in my office or at the bus stop on my way to work as a way to reach out to them and discovered how easy it was to make friends. I was gradually recognizing my importance in the scheme of things and that I always had me to give in any situation. During an evaluation at my job, my boss commented on how much the morale in the office had improved since I had started working there and how I had taken a potentially strained situation between my Self and another employee and changed it for the better. I had a growing sense of contentment as I reached out to others. I was, in fact, causing my own evolution.

From lifetime to lifetime evolution occurs by fulfilling the desires of what we have to give and what we have to learn. When our choices benefit not only ourselves but others as well, then we are well on our way to progressing to the next stage of our spiritual development.

The Past Life Readings are an essential aid and basic prerequisite in the evolution of the spirit of Mankind toward understanding and fulfilling his highest potential. In order to do this, all must honestly face themselves, seeing real strengths and utilizing them to continually greater degrees as well as creating awareness and understandings in the blind spots of the Soul. All must release the inclination to hold back on their dreams. All must give, thus benefiting humanity while fulfilling the individual desires of the soul. Truly both go hand in hand, for in holding back what is being restricted is growth. Giving causes growth to the Whole Self. All must realize that they are not isolated islands but an important part of something greater than any one individually. And all must trust their inner knowing and give from that part of themselves.

We are the ones. Let us move forward.

Born and raised in Oklahoma, Pamela [Carpenter] Blosser received a Bachelor of Arts degree from Texas Christian University with a double major in English and Sociology. In 1969, she embarked on a decade of world-wide travel including living in the Orient for seven of those years. While in Japan, Dr. Pam practiced Zen Buddhism and broadened her studies including skill in the Koto, the Japanese harp. In the late 70's she lived in London where she pursued Montessori certification. Upon returning to the States a year later, Dr. Pam knew she wanted to continue her spiritual studies and began classes in the School of Metaphysics. Since that time she has traveled the Midwest, living in seven major cities where she has taught hundreds of people the course of study offered through the School of Metaphysics.

Now based at the School of Metaphysics Headquarters on the campus of the College of Metaphysics, Dr. Pam serves in many capacities including: instructor in metaphysics and the fine arts, mentor for Spiritual Initiation Sessions, art & production manager for SOM Publishing, and director of the summer college preparatory camp for young people. After earning a Doctorate of Divinity degree in 1994, Dr. Pam became chaplain for the College of Metaphysics. She serves on the Ordination Board of the Interfaith Church of Metaphysics. By 1995 Dr. Pam culminated her formal metaphysical education by receiving a Doctorate in Metaphysics. She is currently writing a book on the topic of Self motivation. Dr. Pam resides with her husband Paul who is assistant campus chaplain and member of the headquarters staff.

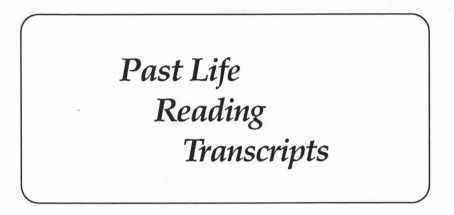

Past Life
Reading
Transcripts

E very reading is significant for the person or people requesting it. A reading reveals the work your soul is here to do. The nature of this work is profoundly personal for it revolves around your present karmic obligations for soul progression. Therefore the information related in a reading can immediately contribute to your spiritual advancement. Knowledge of how the past ties to the present can release you to accomplish what you must, now. This depends upon your willingness to receive, contemplate, assimilate, and utilize the information given. Your life can change because the evolution of your soul is accelerated.

Every reading is also profoundly universal for it is instructive to anyone desiring spiritual growth. This has long been apparent to those of us involved in this research over the past twenty-five years. The universal character of the Truth revealed in these readings offers ancient wisdom for us all in a way that is intriguing and consciousness-expanding. In an effort to share this wisdom and as a means of introducing you to what is revealed in a reading, we have procured permission from several people to print their readings in their entirety. These readings appear, along with remarks from those receiving the readings and commentary by editor Barbara Condron, at the end of each section.

In most cases the questions asked during the reading are included. Although the readings are complete unto themselves, people often have specific questions of particular interest and import to them. The answers usually explain and clarify information given in the body of the reading. By including the questions we hope to offer the novice an idea of the types of questions that are pertinent and that will be answered. For instance a question like "How can I be a better spouse?" will receive a response whereas "Will we get/stay married?" will not. These readings do not predict, although at times they will respond to *possibilities* based upon current conditions in the querent's life. Your future unfolds according to your choices. Since you have free will, you can change the course of your life at any moment. We realize and respect this, therefore, these readings are not fortune telling. They are enlightening glimpses into other realities and how they impact our outward lives.

Thousands of people have benefited from the reading consultations offered through the School of Metaphysics. By sharing just a few of these we hope to enrich life for millions more.

Each Past Life Reading is related in two distinct parts. The first section describes the significant past life. It answers who, where, what, when, and why. The reading will tell you who you were – by name, education, occupation, family, class status, race, religion – whatever facts of your former existence are pertinent to your present lifetime learning. This is the core of what is presented initially. As you will see, the past life part of the reading reads like a short story set in another time and place. But it is not fiction, and this becomes apparent when the connections are drawn between the past lifetime and the present lifetime. Sometimes these connections are linear; the same sex or race, similar familial structure, similar occupations. Sometimes people find they suffered from an affliction or disease in the past life that once again plagues them in the present. These linear similarities are quite astounding when they arise.

Although linear connections are not always present, vertical connections are. Vertical connections are those existing between the outer, physical self and the inner, higher levels of one's consciousness. Within these inner levels, the soul exists and does its work of perfecting. Thus we find an 1800's Caucasian soldier fighting on the side of the Confederacy during the Civil War of the United States, is now a Negro female fighting drug trafficking in a major U.S. city. In this reading, the linear or physical conditions could hardly be more diverse. What is very much connected is the willingness to stand for a belief even when it means risking your physical life.

In the readings that follow you will meet many people, people existing in the present and people who existed at another place in a different time. Whether in their teens or over sixty-five – males and females, professionals and craftsmen, religious and agnostic – they all share a strong conviction to explore, discover, and know what others might take for granted or believe beyond their comprehension. Over the years, readings have been given for people on six continents who are of all races and race-combinations, all religions, all creeds and cultures. The readings are intriguing within themselves but as you study them what will become apparent to you is the universal nature of mankind's experience. Whether pauper or king, everyone is a soul. Every soul is striving toward perfection – a transcendent understanding of creation. The readings reveal where you are in this quest and what you need to be doing to complete the work your soul began lifetimes ago.

In my years of serving as a hostess for those receiving readings, I have many times heard people ask, "When is the Reader going to tell me about my past life?" This is because the information related closely parallels the person's present life; the linear connections. Sometimes this includes many details such as marriage, children, career, even where the person lived. Sometimes the similarity revolves around one striking part of the reading, as was the case with the following reading done for a man who was born in England and who lived many of his adult years in Canada.

You will search for the identity of RB and relate a significant incarnation for this entity.

We see this one in male form and we see this to be in the land area referred to as Sparta. We see for this one to have been highly disciplined and highly rigorously trained through that of the growing years. We see for this to be typical of this time for that of the male sex. We see likewise for this one to place very high demands on the Self for what this one intended to achieve not only within that of the marathon structure, which was intact at this time, but also in terms of becoming that of a lawyer and leader.

We see for this one to take this same rigorous attention as this one demanded of the physical body, and place this upon this one's own sense of accomplishment. We see, likewise, whenever this one fell the least bit short of what this one did demand of the self for this one to fall into periods of strong self-chastisement and strong anger with the self. We see for this one to use this as this one's prime motivation throughout this lifetime.

We see likewise for this one to feel a strong sense of loss of pride whenever this one did fall short of that which this one had intended to achieve. We see for this one to accomplish a great deal, however we see that likewise this one, due to anger, was unable to accept this into the Self and to claim it as this one's own product and this one's own cause. We see therefore for this one to continue to push the self however to set a pattern of exhausting the self through that of the battle situation and through that of the leading process in which this one was involved. We see for this one therefore, especially towards that of this one's latter years, to require extreme periods of recuperation with the attention simply upon relaxing and releasing attention from tension which this one held and kept restrained within this one's own mind.

We see for this one to continue in this pattern. We see for this one to have withdrawn at the age of 32. We see for this one to be referred to as Holst Hyman. We see for this time period to be that of 100 BC.

Did this one marry or have any other relationship during that time period?

We do not see this one to have established that of marital ties. We see for this to have been contradictory to this one's chosen role of that of warrior. We see however for this one to have maintained a defined relationship with that of another female. We do not see for children to be produced.

What would be the significance of that lifetime to the present lifetime for this entity?

We see once again for this one to be very harsh upon the Self in this one's use of anger toward the Self as this one's prime motivator. Suggest that this one likewise to begin placing attention upon building the opposite, that of self-love and self-esteem, an ability to use gentleness with the Self to cause this one to take the precise steps to get where this one does desire. Would suggest to this one that the use of high ideals is not detrimental. What is detrimental is this one's Self-chastisement when this one does not give the Self the proper time or development of growth to achieve this one's ideals. And likewise this one's building impatience which does result in Self-anger. Would suggest this one therefore to build that of the sense of pragmatic gentleness in being able to establish this one's steps toward that which this one does desire in a very clearly defined, practical manner and to be able to cause this one's sense of ideals and expectations of the Self to be realized, piece by piece, with each pragmatic step. This is all. (5-11-82-1-MSR)

"Ancient Greece and the marathons were always fascinating to me," this man commented. "Now I know why.

"(In the present life) I am a Sagittarian (sun sign) and the associated body parts for that astrological influence are the thighs. I understand this to be the desire is for forward motion. Physically, in this lifetime, my legs are well-muscled, and in high school I enjoyed cross-country running a great deal!

"Concerning the more cerebral information, in the present lifetime I have spent considerable time and energy exploring love and this was externally focussed. It made sense to me, especially since I had accepted that the Sagittarian needs to make Self his cause, that now I needed to turn my understanding of love inwards and express love toward my Self.

"Anger has been a thread in the cloth of my life and I can remember as a teenager getting so angry at my mother that I would literally pound the streets of London for three or four hours at a time, in 'marathon' walks. I spent a good deal of the time thinking things through and ended the walking at peace with my mother and within myself. Again, this was a very physical approach to conquering anger. The metaphysical approach was presented to me in this reading. It has given me a different perspective I did not have before, and actively recognizing, then changing, my anger has helped me to control it."

As with anything in life, the information received in a Past Life Reading is only as valuable as the willingness of the recipient to heed, contemplate, resolve, and use the understandings it stimulates. The following reading, although quite different from the one just given, illustrates this point. The readings are similar in that both individuals are angry. What causes the anger and how each understands and resolves the anger is enlightening unto itself.

You will search for the identity known as MM and relate a significant incarnation for this entity.

We see this one in female form. We see the land area to be England. We see that this one was born into a body that did have a disorder that did cause this one's inability to speak. We see that this one did have the ability to make certain sounds but that these were simply guttural sounds and that this one did not have the ability to form any type of words. We see that this was a difficulty in the growing together of this one's palate and roof of the mouth and also a malforming of the sinus cavities. We see that therefore this one did experience much frustration in the early years of this one's life.

We see that this one's parents did have much love for this one but that these ones were very frustrated and guilty at this child having been born with this type of disability and that these ones did not know how to understand what this one was desiring. We see that because of these one's guilt in regards to this child having been born with this deformity these ones did give this one whatever this one demanded. We see therefore that this one did not receive any type of discipline and did become very undisciplined, very angry and very much demanding of attention in whatever ways that this one did desire. We see that many times this was in destructive ways, that this one did learn that by throwing things or by pulling things down or breaking things within this household that this one would be pacified by receiving whatever objects that this one did desire as well as receiving attention from these parents.

We see that this one did continue with these types of behaviors until this one reached the age of five. We see that at this age the ones of the parents became even more distressed and did turn to an institution that was a kind of hospital that had been designed to house children who did have different types of disorders. We see some of these were physical disorders. We see some of these were mental disorders. And we see this one was treated within this institution as if this one was retarded because this one could not speak when in fact this one was highly intelligent. This one's anger and frustration was because of this one's inability to communicate.

We see within this institution this one did become even more undisciplined for this one was very receptive to the thoughts and feelings of those who were around the self. Because of this one's own lack of discipline of this one's own mind, she did become even more susceptible to moods and to emotions. We see within this institution that the ones who were running this institution did not know how to stimulate this one to communicate. We do see that this one did receive a certain kind of discipline, for this one's behavior was not rewarded when it was destructive, but this one was rewarded when this one was more docile. We see therefore this one did learn how to become more quiet and more cooperative for this one did receive rewards in terms of attention and in terms of privileges that this one was given when this one was more cooperative. But this one did not learn how to communicate in more direct ways.

We do see there was another individual who was within this institution who did have some slight retardation but who was intelligent enough to communicate with this one. We see this was an older male. This male did perceive within this one the frustration with the difficulty in communication. We see this male did reach out toward this one, did talk to this one, and did continue to ask this one questions until the male did understand directly what this one did desire. We see the male had learned how to read and how to write, and this male did take this one under his wing and teach this one some elementary forms of speech. We see this did aid this one to a great extent for when this one did have some forms of speech that this one could communicate through writing, this did relieve some of the frustrations but we see that this was not to the extent that this one did need or did desire to fully communicate the thoughts that this one did have.

We see for this one to withdraw at 24 years of age. We see that this was from an overdose that did occur because of this one's curiosity and this one's rebelliousness that this one did ingest this that did cause this one's withdrawal. We see for this one to have been referred to as Nan Schlosser. We see for this time period to be early 1800's.

What understandings were built by this entity in that time period?

We see this one did build understandings of how to manipulate others to fulfill desires. We see this one did begin in the later years of this one's life to learn some about will but that this was not completed.

Very well, what would be the significance of that lifetime to the present lifetime for this entity?

We see within this one there is much anger that this one holds within the self. We see once again that this one does blame others for the anger and that many times this one does not even articulate what is the cause for the anger that this one is experiencing. Would suggest to this one in order for this one to use the anger that is present within the self there is a need for this one to learn how to communicate. Would suggest to this one that in communication this does not simply mean talking. For this one does talk, but we see this one does not listen to the self. Many times this one becomes distracted by this one's own voice and the kind of importance that this one receives from receiving attention from others rather than using this communication as a way of this one identifying this one's thoughts, identifying this one's desires, and then using communication to cause images and plans and some type of concrete action toward the fulfillment of the desires that this one does hold.

It would be suggested to this one to write. It would be suggested that in the use of writing this not only be this one dumping this one's thoughts

but this one learning how to cause there to be form in this one's thinking,
for this one to identify desires within the self and for this one to cause
there to be plans and action taken to fulfill the desires in a very concrete
manner. It would be suggested as well when this one is angry that this
one use this as an indication that there are desires that are being
unfulfilled, and the solution is not for this one to manipulate others into
fulfilling this one's desires but for this one to learn how to fulfill the
desires of the self. This is all. (6-17-91-13-LJF)

Very well, relax.

This woman was taken aback to know she had in effect committed suicide
during the previous life. That was the first of several mental shocks she
received upon hearing her reading. She writes, "It was no surprise to others
that this information came out in my reading. Many of my closest
associates were aware of the simmering anger hovering just below the
surface. Some may have spoken of it to me, but I did not hear them. I had
no idea that anger resided within me and was shocked to learn of this past
life."

As was the case with this lady, some people do not readily accept
the content of their reading. Yet for each of them there are also friends who
recognize the tendencies, whether seething misunderstandings or buried
talents. At first, this woman denied the reading was about her. Yet after
a while the parallels to the present were unmistakable. And the connections
between denial and blame, anger and manipulation, became apparent to
her.

"Once I got past the point of being angry about this reading I was
able to begin the learning process. Notice that I say I was angry at receiving
this reading. At the time I was not aware of the anger. It is only in retrospect
that I remember thinking and saying angry words regarding myself, and
that I laugh at my foolishness. It must have been humorous for others as
they listened to me rant and rave over this past life reading which merely
betrayed the anger the reading was talking about.

"As I listened to the reading over and over again I kept looking for
the anger that was spoken of. Finally, one morning in the shower I heard
my thoughts. I was having yet another mental argument with one of my
authorities. Suddenly, awareness dawned. I did this type of mental arguing
all the time. The inner dialogue was almost constant when I was alone.
There was always a battle going on within me in which someone else

controlled my life and I had to fight for what I wanted.

"This was truly an exciting day for me. Finally I heard my own thoughts and found the truth I had been seeking. Let the healing begin.

"From my perspective communication was something I did quite well. Following a short period of time in denial and angry indignation, I realized that I could learn more. I was humbled. Now it became clear just how much I needed to learn about communication. You know, many times when you think you know it all, something or someone or some situation lets you know that there is still a lot to learn. The insecure ego is put into its proper place and learning is accelerated once again.

"Though it was uncomfortable at first I began talking about my desires. I still feared that I would be misunderstood or that someone would stop me from fulfilling my desires and through my experiences I discovered that it was only I that was stopping me from fulfilling my desires. Once people knew what I wanted they were more than able to aid me in attaining my highest ideals. I learned that the anger was produced from unfulfilled desires – beginning with denial that I had desires and, over time, leading to anger directed toward anything and everything. The cause of my difficulty, lack of communication, was blinding me to the truth. Once I began communicating and fulfilling my desires the anger disappeared and has only reared its head occasionally in the past year.

"I knew that I was unhappy and had been for quite some time and I wanted to change. This stimulated me to obtain this Past Life Reading. Who knows how long it would have taken me to make this change in my thinking and further develop my communication skills without the benefit of knowing what to look for. I am truly grateful for the insights I received from my reading."

I too am grateful for the insights I have received from not only my own readings but the many hundreds I have transcribed or witnessed. I have learned something about myself, about people, about life, about death, about God, about destiny, from every one of them. For instance the previous reading is most instructive in its description of how an unruly and undisciplined child is formed, and how such a child, even when misunderstood and misdiagnosed by well-meaning adults, can be stimulated toward great achievement.

The following reading describes a different kind of parental influence, one with its own set of circumstances and karmic repercussions upon the man, both in the past life and in the present. This Past Life Reading was conducted for a single, middle-aged graphic artist living in the Midwestern United States.

You will search for the identity of the entity referred to as DL and relate a significant incarnation for this entity.

We see this one to be in male form. We see for this to be in Italy. We see that this one was raised in an environment in which there was much isolation. We see that this was in a mountainous area and that this one's family had sporadic contact with other people. We do see that this one spent much time by himself and we see that some of this was outdoors. But we see that much of it was also indoors.

We see that this one tended to spend a great amount of time in fantasy and that this one did attempt to sculpt some of the ideas that this one did have. We do see that this one's father had dabbled in wood carving as a hobby and we see that this one learned this. This one also did experiment with different forms of rock and chisels in order to sculpt.

We see that as this one grew older, this one spent more and more time alone. We do see that this one's mother did encourage this one to associate with other people, but because of the physical conditions these ones lived in, this did require a great amount of effort on this one's part in order to venture outward and to associate with other people. This one found it more comfortable to remain by himself and with his own thoughts. This one did spend more and more time with the sculptures and we see that there were many pieces that this one did craft that were of high quality. We see that this one's mother encouraged this one to sell these, but we see that this one was not concerned with this.

We do see that there were some small ways that this one did have contact with adolescent males. This was through teaching the methods of sculpture that this one had developed. We see that this occurred through this one's mother communicating it with others of her son's talent. We see that this word did spread and there were a few others who did bring their sons to him for education and training. This one did accept these students, but this one did not go out himself in order to solicit them. We do see that this one preferred to spend the time by himself with his own work.

We see for this one to withdraw at 49 years of age. We see that this was from a liver ailment that this one became aware of suddenly. We see for this one to have been referred to as Mario Terizanni. We see for this time period to be early 1800's.

What were this one's thoughts at the point of withdrawal?

We see that this one recognized that this one had gifts, as this one saw it, that this one could have shared but had not.

What would be the significance of that lifetime to the present lifetime for this entity?

We see within this one there is a kind of battle that this one wages in regard to this one's own Self and this one's association with others. We see that this one is rather secretive in regards to this one's real Self. This one therefore tends to cover up who this one is. We see that oftentimes this is unconscious, but we see that there are times when this is very deliberate and this one fears being hurt. Would suggest to this one there is a need for this one to release this one's guard.

We see that there is a need upon this one's part to understand the need for practice in this regard for we see that this one has tended to operate from what is comfortable. Therefore when there is an opportunity for practice – in regard to this one becoming more open and becoming more genuine – this one has not attempted this. Would suggest that the use of visualization would be of great benefit, for we see that this one imagines what would be taken away from the self or what this one needs to protect rather than this one imagining the benefits that this one will receive from being more genuine and more open and more sincere.

What are the benefits that this one will receive from those qualities?

The primary benefit is that this one will discover who he is. We see that this one tends to be rather unconscious of who he is inwardly. Would suggest to this one to imagine how this one can be more open and for this one to practice this.

What is meant by "open"?

For this one to be himself, for this one to remove the attention from how this one will be received or accepted, and to simply give based upon the needs of the individuals around this one. We do see that stilling the mind would benefit this one in order for this one to perceive the needs of others rather than being habitual about how this one relates. (11-2-95-3-LJC)

Upon receiving his reading, the man had this to say, "After hearing the first couple of sentences of this reading, I knew instantly what the whole reading encompassed. Several of the other readings I had received over the years had indicated a need for me to be more open with others. In a sense, I was frustrated with what the current reading was telling me, but I knew it contained a lesson I needed to learn.

"The reading was very accurate in identifying my attitudes at the time of the reading. I knew that I had to release my guard as the reading suggested. In my [work] position, it is imperative that I be open and willing to receive people into my life if I am to fulfill my reason for being in this position. I very much desire to give of my knowledge to humanity. The reading instilled in me more determination to learn this lesson of being more open.

"As I thought about this reading more and more I began to be more honest with myself. I could clearly see how I had been insincere with some people in my life and how I had shut them out this way. I obtained this reading because I felt 'stuck' in my current situation. It helped me more clearly identify what my next step is and for that I am thankful."

The transcribing of readings has been carried on by students of the School of Metaphysics for years. This is considered a major part of their education, partly because the nature of the material is unique and partly because its content is fertile with wisdom and the workings of the Universal Laws. In this reading the suggestions to understand and create openness in Self can be applied by anyone to enhance the quality of life. For those wanting to understand karmic obligations, you can readily see how this man's dependence upon his mother to "advertise" his better qualities in the previous life has left him ill-equipped in the present to interact with others. Again this man tends to wait for others to provide him with a place to give rather than creating the place for himself. His primary karmic obligation becomes apparent. The self-initiative to give is still lacking in this soul, hence this particular past lifetime is relevant to the present. Rather than continue to repeat the same patterns or imagine himself a victim of other's rejection, the man can now take control of himself and his life.

These readings will always identify karmic indentures and offer suggestions to deepen understanding and heighten awareness of self and our relationships with others. Many times they answer questions held in the mind for years. Sometimes they will offer insights into intuitive inklings that have arisen seemingly without cause. Significant Past Life Readings can offer an explanation into thoughts, inclinations, or urges that do not arise from the conscious mind. For instance, deja vu experiences often are snippets of memory extending far beyond the present lifetime recall stored in the brain. This ethereal memory is not of the physical, it is of the soul. One woman discovered the meaning of an experience she had had years before while visiting a foreign country:

We see this one in female form. We see this to be in England. We see for this one to be raised in a very traditional household and we see that this one was taught certain duties in cooperating with this one's family. We see this was with the expectation that this one would marry and have her own family. We see this one received the kinds of educational skills and training that would prepare this one to be a wife and mother. We see for this one to be dutiful.

We see, however, that this one oftentimes retreated into this one's imagination because we see this one did aspire to become something more and greater than what was expected of this one. We see this one did have brothers who attended formal schooling and we see that this one did learn from them how to read and write. We see this one kept a journal and this one did record her experiences. We see this one did also sketch and we see there was a kind of storybook that this one put together of her life and her experiences with the illustrations. We see this one kept this private and we see this one did use this for an outlet for her imagination. We see that this did provide a stimulus for this one.

We see this one married. We see this one had four children. We see this one did tell stories to the children. This one did also use this one's artistic creativity in different kinds of crafts and different kinds of projects that this one pursued with the children. We do see that this one did continue to keep a journal and for the most part this was kept secret although we do see some of the stories this one did share with her children. This one's husband was aware of the journal that this one kept but we see the one of the husband did think this was simply a pastime. He did not understand the significance to this one of this.

We see that once the ones of the children were grown, this one became very bored. We see this one did desire for there to be a greater outlet of expression. We see, however, that this one did not formulate any kind of expression for the Self and we see that this one did withdraw [from the physical, meaning died]. *We see this was when this one was 42 years of age. We see that this was from a stroke. We see for this one to have been referred to as Amy Tanner. We see for this time period to be 1700's.*

Very well, what would be the significance of that lifetime to the present lifetime for this entity?

We see within this one there is a conflict of interest that does arise. We see there is a conservative nature that this one has. We see there are certain ideals that this one holds within the Self concerning what is right, what is proper, what is expected and what is valuable. We see that many of these ideas have substance and value, but we see this one needs to give greater attention to these and to give greater thought to the purpose for these ideas and ideals for we do see that oftentimes this one becomes habitual in this one's activity. We see that rather than this one understanding the true purpose for these ideas and values, this one operates by a kind of rule bound nature.

We see that the conflict arises when this one has desires for expansion for creative thinking, for creative activity, for moving the Self beyond the bounds of what this one has experienced. We see this one views this as a conflict and this one views these ideas and ideals as being contradictory.

Would suggest to this one that in order for this to be resolved and in order for these ideas to come together, there is a need for purposeful thinking. There is a need for this one to consider what is universally true. We see this would aid this one in making choices on a day-to-day basis. We see there is a need for this one to consider the ways in which she wants to expand the Self and in which she wants to cause the Self to grow rather than simply thinking of expansion as being different activities in life. The true expansion that this one seeks is for this one's own growth and for this one's transformation. This is all.

At times I have a lot of anxiety about money. What is the cause of this?

We see that this one has not learned about the universal principles of creation that would enable this one to have the security of knowing that this one can create and fulfill this one's physical needs. Would suggest to this one that this is one area that this one would benefit from focusing upon the kind of Self growth, Self transformation and Self understanding that this one desires to learn rather than upon the physical condition itself.

We see also it would benefit this one to discriminate between needs and wants and for this one to focus upon fulfilling this one's needs rather than fearing that this one will not be able to satisfy every want that this one could imagine.

How can I deepen my meditation?

The first step would be for this one to dedicate the Self to concentrating. We see that this one does have information and knowledge concerning this but we see there is a need for greater commitment and greater dedication to causing the mind to be still.

How can I improve speaking what is on my mind?

For this one to determine that this one will do this and then to image this and then to follow through with the activity.

How can I advance and excel in my career?

It would benefit this one to formulate an image of who this one wants to be. Formulating an image of who this one wants to be would provide a clear image to this one of the kind of influence that this one can have and this would be the means by which this one would advance. (1-12-94-5-LJF)

"I have had several readings from the School of Metaphysics," this woman said. "This reading struck true to my heart. One thing that impressed me immediately was related to an experience I had in 1988. I was traveling alone through England. I had spent a few days south of London in a beautiful and peaceful town. One day in particular I was out on a long walk through the countryside. I had my journal with me as was my practice. I stopped many times to record my thoughts and feelings. What was unusual was that I had an overwhelming desire to draw in my journal that day. I did not consider myself an artist and I never sketched anything in my journal.

I did sit down and draw pictures of the landscape and a few abstract pictures. Then as I wrote afterwards I speculated why I was so compelled to sketch. I pondered at that point the possibility of a past life in England. Little did I know that six years later that past lifetime in England would mean so much to me.

"I used the information in this reading in many ways. First and foremost I created a clear picture of who I wanted to become in relation to my career. I am a massage therapist and was starting a new business in a new town. I wrote out clear descriptions of how I wanted to aid my clients, what type of therapist I wanted to be and steps I would take to accomplish this. Within one month I had a regular base of clients and business was growing steadily.

"I recognized some of the areas that I was habitual in my thinking and actions. I began to give much deeper thought to what I was doing, why and how I could further my growth as a result. This aided me greatly to ease the inner conflict that I experienced when I thought that my ideas and ideals did not match up."

The sense of being in charge of your own destiny is just one of the benefits derived from a Past Life Reading. Another benefit is the stunning clarity of insight from a point of cause. Past Life Readings cut through extraneous factors that can cloud issues and blind the individual to the whys of life. When we cannot identify the causal thought from which our problem arises, we are ill-equipped to resolve difficulties. This promotes the cycle of blaming and victimization so prevalent in society. Yet as we have witnessed particularly in the United States this cycle is a malaise. Healing can only occur as society demands individual responsibility from its citizens. Where there is individual responsibility there is group responsibility. And where there is responsibility there is freedom.

The identification of a causal thought is an enlightening experience. I know because I have experienced it each time I review and contemplate the first Past Life Reading I received from the School back in the mid-1970's. This information empowered me to more fully understand my own motivations. It also prepared me to determine the course my life would take – and indeed has taken – in a way nothing else had to that point:

You will search for the identity of the entity known as BGO and relate a significant incarnation for this entity.

We see this one as female. This one is in a temple of religious worship for the people. We see this is not only a religious worship but representing a type of lifestyle, an attitude or ideals that are considered and used in every aspect of life. We see this one to have been chosen to work within this temple and to study the concepts brought forth within this temple. We see this one to have been greatly honored in this and to take great pride in this position; to be very enthusiastic and to attempt to project this enthusiasm to others.

We see this to involve a certain disciplinary procedure which requires great attention being placed upon certain areas and we see this one to pursue this with great diligence and enthusiasm. We see the purpose set forth in this activity to be the enlightenment of other individuals and the building forth within Self the complete enlightenment and unfoldment of the lower self to the higher. We see this one to pursue these studies to reach a point where this one was able to disperse this information to other individuals. We see this one to view this passing on of information as a great responsibility and to be overly concerned with this one's doing this in a correct manner, and therefore, after great inner turmoil and much time spent in arriving at a decision, we see this one to withdraw from these temple duties and to withdraw from this study for this one felt the lack within Self to adequately demonstrate these qualities and project the proper information to others as this one would see to be in a perfect manner. We see this one to be very distraught over doing things in what would be considered a perfect way instead of doing things in a manner which is to the best of her abilities.

We see this one at that point to direct Self in a way which this one would consider herself to be creative, in the ways of art and music. We see this one to express these spiritual ideals in this manner, in the creation of art forms and in carvings and also in playing music. We see this one to find great pleasure and release of anxieties through these two forms. We see also this one to be somewhat disturbed within Self for not living up to what would be considered perfection.

We see this one to not marry within this lifetime, but to form a companionship with many other entities and to share much of the enthusiasm and joy this one finds in the expression of physical life. We see this one to continue in this manner until the time of withdrawal. We see this to be age 58 years. We see this to be an area of the Mayan people in Central America.

How was this time period referred to?

There is not a time period given.

How was this entity referred to?

Quaradon.

Is this the only name?

Yes.

What type of religion did this one follow?

We see this religion as being the worship of one particular God or deity, and this being represented in certain symbology. We see also there to be other deities which would be considered lesser in effect in status which are represented by smaller stones. We see there to be much symbology represented within this religious practice and this to not be clear to all individuals. We see this one to have reached only a certain point in understanding the representation of this symbology and not to have continued beyond this point due to the qualities that have been given.

Do you find the one of Quetzecoatl as being at this time?

Not existing during this time period, but representative in the religious ideals of the period.

Was there a particular reason why this entity did not marry in that lifetime, take a mate?

This one had many companions for brief periods, did not choose to remain with any of them for a long duration. This is due to this one's feeling – not feeling – a need to do this. As stated, this one had developed an independence which was not in accordance with remaining with one male for a long extended period.

Did this entity have children?

There was one male child.

Did this child live and grow up to adulthood?

There was a separation of this child from this one when the child was small. This one did not raise the child.

What was the reason for this entity not raising the child?

The child was given to another to raise during the period when this one sought to express Self in the religious attitude that has been given.

What would be the significance of that lifetime to the present lifetime for this entity?

We see this one presently to also have a desire to reach out to others and to pass on to them the knowledge and experience this one has reached, and to do this in such a way as to always express with enthusiasm and a positive attitude to where these will respond and recognize the value of those things that this one seeks to give. We see this one to have some degree of insecurity in doing this and this to relate primarily with the purpose this one has sought in choosing this lifetime and this time period. We see this to be an extension of desire that has not been fulfilled in the past and the need at the present time to completely express during the present period. We see this one to have formed a great deal of strength and independence from the past, and to still find the need to express Self in this way, and to do this in such a way as to further the purpose and goals this one has set forth for Self.

Would suggest to this one that there is no need for this one to feel insecure, for the finding of security in what this one presents is gained through experience and this one is in the process of forming this. Suggest to this one to see Self in the positive manner that this one projects to other individuals, for through this and through the continuous application of those principles received, this one will form the security this one requires and will be able to share with others in the proper approach.

We see this one also to have an error in attitude regarding the perfection of Self in all activities. Would suggest to this one that perfection is not required in experience upon the earth plane, but only the performing of the activity to the best of one's ability. Therefore, do not deny Self the right to make errors, for errors can be valuable learning tools. This is all. (10-10-75-7-JMW)

I was astounded.

The reading was accurate.   At least the information in the significance was accurate, I was at first undecided about the past life part. The reader had not met me before giving me this reading. It was as if she had read my thoughts, describing those which I believed I held secret, while revealing others I was not as yet conscious.

Upon first hearing the reading, I could understand why this particular past incarnation was significant: the religious upbringing, the deep sense of spirituality, the applied study, the art and music. All were applicable to my present life, not so much in a linear, doing-the-same-thing fashion but in the tone, scope, and implications described. For instance in the past lifetime I left my family to enter the temple, in my present life my grandfather – an evangelist – lived with our family throughout most of my childhood. The circumstances between the two lives were different but the result was the same: religious faith was a major part of my early training and became a part of my moral fiber and character.

The past life covered an entire lifetime, my present lifetime was only 22 years at the time I received this reading so many of the significances were probabilities. For instance, the past couplings and child were a result of how I previously lived a full life. In the present, I had recently broken an engagement to my high school sweetheart, had no children, and was not yet interested in coupling.   I had however always wanted to be a teacher – indeed had pretended to be one as a child – and was at the time of receiving the reading considering teaching metaphysics. I would find in the months and years to follow that the same challenges described in this reading would arise in my present-day efforts to learn to teach with mastery. There were several times I wavered in my dedication, wondering if the love for what I was doing was strong enough to meet the labor, just as I had done in that Mayan period.   At those times this reading served as a stimulus for perspective, objectivity, insight, and motivation to meet my limitations and move beyond them.

This reading was profoundly significant to me. It has helped me identify unknown factors in my life that would have eluded me otherwise. It has helped me to learn and change my own sense of identity or ego, freeing me to mature in judgement and wisdom. It continues to benefit me now almost 25 years later. And I can perceive my progress. It's like tying up loose ends that have existed for centuries. The sense of filling the soul is acutely real.

I have through the years been present for, transcribed, and had the honor of giving literally thousands of readings. Although not all Past Life Readings are as encompassing as my first reading proved to be, I have found all Past Life Readings are immediately relevant in pinpointing karmic obligations which need a response. Because readings are significant to the individual now, they at the very least offer an opportunity to admit and cease self-defeating patterns of thought and behavior and at the most bring the opportunity for great vision that can lead to enlightenment.

The recounting of a past life often sounds like the screenplay for a movie. But these readings are descriptions of what has occurred, not what is imagined. For this reason, Past Life Readings offer a unique and often detailed review of history. From the building of the pyramids to early acupuncture, from the invention of musical instruments to study under any one of the world's great spiritual masters, you can find mankind's history in these readings. Outstanding in this regard is the information on Atlantis. These readings reveal Atlantis to be more than a physical place. They describe Atlantis as a group of people and a time period in man's history as well. The following reading is an example of an Atlantean reading.

On a more personally relevant level, this reading also illustrates how a soul can and does experience in one lifetime as a female and in another as a male. Although an alien concept to those who identify only with the physical body, from the perspective of the soul the potential for understanding is paramount, not the sex of the body used to gain those understandings. The same is true for someone who is Mongoloid this lifetime and was Negroid or Caucasoid in prior lives, or a Russian who discovers s/he was Chinese or Mexican or Nigerian in another life time. What makes these readings significant to the person receiving them is similar attitudes which determines the karmic factors and parallel learning opportunities which offer the chance for soul progression. Sometimes the soul's need for advancement overrides the relativity of the soul's choice of body such as in the following reading where the inquirer is now female and was male in the past life.

You will search for the essence of the entity known as LF and relate a significant incarnation for this entity.

We see this one in male form. We see this one to be within the area referred to as Atlantis. We see for this one to be affiliated with the group of people who were considered the older faction or those who had vision and foresight. We see for this one to effect a type of teaching position. We see for this one, however, to become very immersed and emotionally involved in working with the other individuals.

We see for there to be many of a newer faction who were quite dissatisfied. We see for there to be experimentations which were occurring in regards to the physical form and we see for there to be manipulation of energies which this one became involved in and we see for there to be the knowledge within this one of repercussions or many of the effects of what was being produced at that time. We see this one to find great frustration in the Self of attempting to convey this to the ones of the others.

We see for this one to begin doubting his own knowledge. We see for there to be such pressure placed upon this one through the emotional involvement of those who were experimenting that this one became more and more engrossed in the emotional reactions, not only of the others, but also his own. We see this one eventually ceased this teaching, this attempt to teach, due to the lack of trusting the Self, trusting his own vision, his own knowledge, his own perception. We see during this period for there to be a withdrawal into the Self, and we see for this to last a long period of time. We see during this time for this one to attempt to reconcile this, however, we see this one not to offer the Self opportunities to work with this attitude and to change it. We see this one to desire to do this merely as a mental exercise and we see that there was not the practicing of the theories that this one would develop.

We see for this one during the later time period to begin perceiving events. We see for this one to find these so horrifying, for they carried with them devastations, that this one attempted once again, for the first time in a long period of time, to alert other individuals to it. We see, however, once again this one to meet with the rejection. We see, however, this time for this one not to falter or not to withdraw into the Self but to continue until the time of withdrawal in attempting to alert other individuals to this. We see this to be within the fourth cycle of Atlantis. We see this one referred to as Plantiva. This is all.

What would be considered the age of withdrawal for this entity in this time period?

Would be 31 years of age.

Would you be more specific about how this entity manipulated energies?

We see this one not to be directly involved in that. We see for this to be observed by this one and to be done by the younger faction who had very little experience in this regard. We see for this one to be in a teacher capacity within this group of people; however, we see for the group of people to begin going off on an entirely different tangent which this one could see would be destructive in nature or less than beneficial.

What would be the significance of that lifetime to the present lifetime for this entity?

We see once again there is the need within this one to begin trusting the Self to a greater extent. We see this one allows the environment to influence the Self to such an extent at times that this one loses her own perspective and her own perception. We see this one to have great perception in many cases and to have a good sense of vision of being able to see lines of probability. Would suggest to this one to begin appreciating this and using it.

Would suggest that there is the tendency within this one, once again, to withdraw into the Self when there is a mistake made or there is error seen in this one's presentation. Would suggest, however, that each period of withdrawal into the Self merely elongates the period of time that this one would impose upon the Self in coming to a conclusion or resolving this within the Self. Would suggest this one merely begin to consistently initiate activity in regards to what this one desires to accomplish.

Are there any further suggestions as to activity rather than to withdraw within the Self?

Would suggest immediately upon recognizing this in the Self to make a decision to take action. Would suggest that this could come in movement of the physical body, in words, in any type of activity. Would suggest, however, that there is the need within this one at this time not to begin placing so much attention upon the physical activity, the physical results, that this one loses sight of the validity and the reality of mental activity. Would suggest this one begin using all that is available. (9-7-80-7-BGO)

The personal value of this reading stimulated this woman to alter the course of her life. She used this information to overcome her own inertia and has since become a respected authority in several fields. In addition to teaching and guest speaking, she is often interviewed by the media and is a published writer.

The woman who had this reading commented on its value to her: "When I first heard this reading I was amazed, but not exactly shocked. As soon as I heard it I knew it was true; it resonated deep within me and images from my present-day life flashed up in my mind relating to the significance of the reading.

"At the time of the reading, I had already made significant strides in committing myself to teaching and sharing the metaphysical knowledge I had learned with others. I was the director of a school of higher learning and teaching others. Often, I experienced situations in which I presented truth to my students or gave them instructions and they told me I was wrong. Although somewhere deep within myself I believed that what I said was true, I began to doubt myself. Especially when I encountered students who were very vehement and convinced of their own opinions, I would think, 'Maybe I'm crazy.' This was an old way of thinking; ever since I was a child I had encountered other people who were opinionated and who voiced their thoughts strongly. My habit was to withdraw and remain silent, or to doubt myself, especially if I was alone in my way of thinking. Often throughout my life I had thought that I might be crazy because my ideas were different from others. It made perfect sense to me that in that past lifetime I was part of the older group with foresight and vision. In this lifetime I had frequently been ahead of my peer group in school, was often attracted to adults rather than children for conversation, and many times had ideas that were uncommon and visionary.

"This reading helped me become more honest and to respond to what deep down inside I wanted to believe: that it was not that I was crazy. I really did have valid perceptions and the lines of probability I could perceive were accurate. The need for me to 'stick to my guns' and present truth whether other people agreed with it or not became apparent. Most significant to me was the suggestion offered about what to do rather than withdrawing into myself. I was aware of that tendency, and although I didn't like it, sometimes I didn't know what to do when I felt myself withdrawing into extreme introspection. The suggestion to do something, any kind of activity, was very helpful. It gave me something concrete to *do* in order to practice a different kind of thinking. Rather than being an intellectual exercise, the reading provided valuable insight for me to make changes that I had been needing and wanting to make for many years."

The universal value of this reading, and others during the Atlantean time period, is astounding. Little recorded history remains of this civilization beyond a mention in the writings of Plato or the intuitive work of Edgar Cayce. Our readings indicate this would not be so had the libraries at Alexandria been spared from destruction. When physically recorded history is lacking, memory is the only means for retaining and retelling the stories of the past. This is true in the present for you, your parents, your grandparents, your physical heritage. And it is true for the soul which has experienced the earthly plane many times in an effort to learn, understand, and reach fulfillment.

Just as physical libraries exist as a source of recorded history, so the Akashic Record serves as a mental library on the inner planes of existence. The outstanding difference is the availability in the Record of information on *everything,* both thought and action, that has occurred in the past. The opportunities for research, study, and insight are boundless. We at the School of Metaphysics are presently seeking funding to catalogue, cross-reference, and computerize the volumes of readings done over the past decades. We hope to make this information widely available around the world in the coming century. We believe it will accelerate mankind's spiritual evolution.

Part II

Past Life Crossing of Paths Readings

"The opinions which we hold of one another,
our relations with friends and kinsfolks,
are in no sense permanent, save in appearance,
but are as eternally fluid as the sea itself."

—*Marcel Proust (1913)*

L ooking back on it now, Crystal says she must have been fourteen years old. Her grandmother was suffering from Parkinson's disease and very ill. She tended to hallucinate, talking about things that didn't really happen or people who didn't exist.

The woman's family visited her and during the entire conversation the young girl curiously noted that the grandmother referred to her son, Crystal's father, by the name *Robert*. The man corrected his mother on several occasions reminding her that his name was Gary, not Robert. Later grandmother took Crystal aside and told the girl that she had been a good wife to Robert.

For years, like everyone else, Crystal believed her grandmother's last words were merely the ramblings of a feverish brain filled with sickness.

"I didn't know what she was saying until years later when I received a Past Life Crossing with my father. The crossing revealed that my father and I had indeed been married in a prior lifetime, and his name had been — *Robert*! Now I understood what my grandmother was trying to tell me so many years ago. I just didn't know how to listen and understand. It also explained why my relationship with my father this lifetime was very different from the ones he had with my sisters. And that was an answer I had been seeking for as many years."

As is so often the case, this significant past life information was not only pertinent to the woman's present relationship with her father, but also shed new light on her earlier experience with her grandmother. It explained why the girl's relationship with her present-day father was quite different from the one he shared with her two sisters. It also confirmed her grandmother's state of mind during her final days, verifying her intuitive perception.

Consciously we yearn for wholeness. We reach toward others for love, friendship, companionship, stimulation, communion, challenge.

We need others to reflect our strengths and weaknesses, to share our aspirations and hopes, to serve and to lead. By developing relationships with others we come to know ourselves, inwardly as well as outwardly. The people we choose to associate with reveal our values and principles, our understanding of life and our lack of it.

The inner, subconscious mind can be likened to a puzzle. The outlining form of the puzzle becomes the guideline used to enter puzzle pieces. This outline is stored in the soul as a reflection of the blueprint for your maturation as a Spiritual Being. As the cause of each experience in the physical life is identified, understood, and made a part of Self, you discover a piece of your puzzle that will fit into the outlining form. The need for incarning into physical life will continue until your puzzle is completed.

At this stage of Man's evolution most of the puzzle can be perceived, thus we find talents and abilities that we did not learn in this lifetime making themselves known. As you draw upon what you have already made a part of your Self, you demonstrate genius. Talent garnered in past lifetimes often becomes apparent in the present by what we give to and receive from others. The Past Life Crossings offer deep insight into what subconscious forces are at work in our relationships. They describe the nature and reason for attraction, or avoidance. They teach us that no one is a stranger, for in so many cases the people we now associate with are souls we have known before. Crossings paint a picture of two souls pursuing their spiritual quests, who meet and travel together for a time. How the journeying together enriches them as individuals is a bond that transcends physical time. It is the fate that brings people together.

To insure that spiritual evolution continues, the Universal Law of Cause and Effect operates in our lives as what is known as karma. *Karma* is a Sanskrit word meaning *act* or *fate–that which has been spoken.* To have the ability to know what your karmic obligations are and to add understanding of these to your Self, is to complete your soul's puzzle. And this is the real work of the soul. By relating to and with others, we stimulate the realization of the work we are here to do.

Past Life Crossing of Paths bring these karmic indentures clearly into focus, giving us a way to live more fully. And perhaps more importantly, they offer the understanding that love transcends the limits of a physical lifetime into yesterday and perhaps into tomorrow as well.

Crossing of Paths Readings
by Paul Blosser, B. A.

Have We Met Before?

Bruce was my best friend in the seventh grade. I was a ninety-five pound weakling, Bruce was twenty pounds lighter. I approached Bruce in the hallway on the second day of school, just after we left algebra class.

"Hey, aren't you in my fourth hour history class?" I asked, attempting to strike up a conversation. From that moment on, we were friends. We ate gruel together in the school cafeteria. We shot spit wads during history class while the teacher's head was turned. We both detested gym class when we learned square dancing and had to touch girls.

We read *MAD Magazine* from cover to cover and we doodled endlessly. Bruce could draw the greatest Rat Finks with their tongues hanging out and driving the weirdest cars. His *piece-de-resistance* was Snoopy the flying ace piloting his bullet-ridden Sopwith Camel and cursing the Red Baron.

We liked the same kinds of books and swapped library books back and forth. We liked fiction stories about heroes like Captain Nemo, biographies of great men like Harry Houdini, Thomas Edison, and Old Hickory. We consumed stories of adventure and intrigue. In fact, we created a wonderful Walter Mitty intrigue of our own. In our fantasy, we were heroes. One night, while most of the United States slumbered, the Communists bombed us and thousands of troops parachuted in and took over. Only Bruce and I could save democracy and the United States! Given the reality of 1967 and the creative genius of two teenage boys, we began making concrete plans–just in case! Bruce had some pretty wicked ideas about his pellet gun that also shot darts. We'd also break into sporting goods stores and steal ammunition and rifles. We'd make Malatov cocktails (I had to ask Bruce what they were) and build our own bombs. We developed our own secret code and tested it passing notes in history class. We plotted the best places to attack the enemy and planned ways to trap them.

Bruce and I enjoyed each other's company. It seemed like we'd laugh forever when we were together. Our imaginations were stimulated endlessly, by each other, by the books we read and the movies we saw, by the jokes we told and by the "cracked" perspective we shared on life, junior high school, and girls.

Our friendship and shared experiences grew during that two year period, seeded from an instant mutual attraction. I felt comfortable with Bruce the first time I saw him, almost as if I knew we would be friends before I ever talked to him.

You've probably had similar experiences of meeting someone for the first time and becoming best friends right away, as if you'd known each other all your life, or perhaps lifetimes. You find out that you have many of the same interests, perhaps similar backgrounds and experiences, common likes and dislikes.

You can probably recall a relationship that started with the mutual attraction of love at first sight. Or perhaps you'd describe your relationship to a person of the same sex as "sisterly love" or "he's just like the brother I never had". Your attraction to an older man might be attributed to the qualities you see in your father or grandfather. If asked to describe these types of attractions you would probably use physical or emotional terms. Yet this is only two-dimensional, like trying to describe a kitchen table in two dimensions; the table is three feet wide and thirty-two inches high. You have no idea how long the table is and whether you can seat four at your dinner party or twenty-four.

Although we are physical and emotional beings, we are also mental or spiritual beings. Incorporating the mental and spiritual perspective to a relationship is the third dimension of the relationship, just like adding the third dimension to our kitchen table! It is this third dimension to our relationships that explains what this mutual, instant attraction is and how it works. This added dimension adds depth to the relationship.

If you consider the physical laws of nature, such as the law of gravity or the law of magnetic attraction, then you can begin to understand the Universal or Mental Law of Attraction. Each of the mental laws are explained by universal truths; "what goes up, must come down" explains the law of gravity. Our Mental Law of Attraction could be explained as "like attracts like" or, more precisely, "you will attract to you the people, places, and things that will offer you the greatest learning opportunities."

Like the laws in nature, the mental laws are impartial. These laws are always at work, for anyone, anytime, anyplace. You can demonstrate and experience the law of gravity at any time by dropping a pencil or sitting under an apple tree like Sir Isaac Newton supposedly did. You can experience the mental law of attraction by going to a movie or the grocery store, wherever and whenever people gather with a common goal.

So this concept of Universal Law and Universal Truth doesn't seem so far-fetched. If I go to the movie theater, everyone there has a desire to see the same movie. It makes sense that the people in my life are part of my life for a reason, that there is some common mental ground far more important than watching a movie.

This mental "real" attraction that draws us together is what manifests as the physical attraction or the emotional attraction. Although there are only a finite number of ways for a relationship to exist in our physical world such as husband and wife or lovers, as best friends, as business partners, the mental dynamics and possibilities of any relationship are as unique as the individuals involved.

What about the saying that "opposites attract"? The mental law of attraction still works, but what might appear dissimilar from the outside is built around common learning opportunities. Two people in a relationship may have diverse interests and backgrounds. Together, these two "halves" make a whole. Each person brings unique qualities and interests to the relationship. Have you ever dated someone who expanded your interests beyond baseball to music, art to science? Your partner can stimulate you to gain new experiences. Two friends, John and Laurel, illustrate how opposites attract and complement each other. Laurel enjoys literature, writing, and art while John's interests lie in team sports and golf. In relating to each other, they use the diversity in interests to try new experiences while sharing common goals. This stimulation and sharing is at the heart of all productive relationships with others.

Spirals of Growth

While I was in college, I dated a woman who was several years younger than I. She had never been married. I had been divorced and was a single parent. We dated for three years and talked about marriage and about creating our own advertising and public relations firm.

This had been a case of instant attraction. She attended a college in Louisville and returned to visit a friend, my neighbor, during spring break one year. We became friends and when she moved back to Oklahoma for the summer, we began dating. In the fall, she transferred to the University of Oklahoma where I was enrolled, so we could be together. During the next three years we were virtually inseparable.

She was struggling to be independent. Although she wanted to live her own life, she depended on her parents to pay her college expenses. I was trying to figure out what I wanted to do with my life. I'd set a goal two years earlier to finish a military career but medical conditions changed those plans.

In many ways, each of us had our future tied up in our relationship. I was a means for her to rebel against her parents since they didn't exactly approve of me, and she was my hope of a future. We built a dependency on each other as to who we were and what we wanted. I came to know that my identity was built around our relationship.

After we broke up, I was severely depressed and angry, and I took my anger out on the people in my world. It took many months for me to reestablish my own Self image and begin to see that I could accomplish what I wanted to with my life.

Each of us dealt with the breakup of that relationship. We didn't have the benefit of knowing how we could have more fully used the relationship as individuals while it was in progress. I had yet to learn about the School of Metaphysics and the service of Past Life Crossings.

I hadn't been studying metaphysics long when I heard about the Past Life Readings and Past Life Crossings. From a purely scientific and physical standpoint the idea that I had lived before made sense, after all the body I was using consisted of a small universe of atomic particles, electrons, protons, and neutrons. I knew that from eighth grade science class. I was a bundle of electrical energy and would always be in some form or another so the idea that I had been a physical human being before was not far-fetched. I also knew that I had a soul, but I had no concept of how or if it fit into the idea of reincarnation.

In fact, I didn't have that much of an idea about what reincarnation was. I knew that people in India believed in reincarnation. They believed someone died and came back as a cow. That part didn't make sense to my Western mind! It seemed preposterous that once I had achieved the status of a human being I would want to go backwards, expressing in what I considered a lower life form.

I decided to satisfy my curiosity and after some discussion with my teacher and school director, I decided to have a Past Life Crossing with my daughter, Michelle. She was ten at that time and I was a single parent. The school director told me the reading would reveal a significant past association Michelle and I had shared. She said Michelle and I had probably been together many times, and the reading would relate an association most closely matching our current relationship. She said the reading would aid our relationship and help me be a better parent.

As the reading session began, I was intrigued, nervous, and skeptical. After all, I was new to this and I barely knew these people. In fact, I had never met the woman who was reading the mysterious Akashic Records. The Reader and Conductor sat next to each other in the living room. A small table with cassette tapes and two tape players sat in front of the Conductor. Several observers and the people having readings crowded into the living room area, sitting on sofas and straight-backed kitchen chairs. A lone chair sat empty in front of the Reader and Conductor for the person receiving the reading. The Conductor began preparing the Reader for the session.

Once the session began, the Conductor looked at me and said, "Paul Blosser". I got up and moved to the empty chair. I knew that no one would see my sweaty palms, but I was afraid they would see my hands shaking.

"You will search for the identity of the entity referred to as Paul Gerald Blosser," instructed the Conductor. "You will search for a significant crossing of paths with this one referred to as Paul Gerald Blosser and that one referred to as Michelle Laura Blosser, and relate that significant crossing."

The Reader related that Michelle and I had been husband and wife in Germany in the late 1600's. Through my family trade, I was very adept (and stubborn) at my work in the garment industry. Michelle was a seamstress although she loved to care for and heal animals.

Okay, I could see how part of this could be true. There were many similarities between the past and present though some of them were what I considered vague. Michelle had a dog named Fuzzy and she loved him, taking good care of him. I had learned as a child to sew. In fact, I had just given Michelle a quilt for Christmas that I had made. I liked German food and studied German in college, but I figured this was because my family had been stationed in Germany when my father was in the Air Force.

I could also see that Michelle and I occupied similar roles within our association. Michelle had particular duties in caring for our home such as folding the laundry, doing the dishes, and vacuuming. And I had my prescribed duties as the head of the household such as paying the bills, cooking, and yard work.

The Reader stated that in our past association I believed in order and structure in life, living by rules and standards about how, when, and why things should be done as they were supposed to be done. Michelle however brought constant, spontaneous changes to our lifestyle which were very upsetting to me. Although this caused resentment in me, Michelle felt torn between her duty to me and her duty to the people in the community.

Part of this made sense to me. As the parent, there were certain rules and regulations I insisted upon; bedtime was 10 p.m. on school nights, homework and chores needed to be completed before playing, and Michelle was to ask permission to go to someone's house or to shop with a friend and parent so I knew who she was with and where she could be found.

> *"We see upon the part of the female that this one had a very great love for the one of the male, but we see that at the same time, this one felt as though this one owed those ones that came to this one for service. We see that this one saw the self as being torn between the wants and the demands of the husband and the needs of others within the community. We see however this one gave very little attention to this one's own needs and how each could satisfy the needs on the part of the Self." (1-9-88-5-GBM)*

The reading revealed that in her past life Michelle's perception was one of sacrificing what she wanted so she could meet the demands of the husband and the demands of the villagers. Her resentment and frustration concerning this continued throughout that lifetime. Communication was a primary issue to be resolved between us in the past.

> *"We see that these ones continued in primarily the same manner throughout that period of time. We see that there were ways where the one of the male was constantly wanting something from the female, that this one was constantly trying to achieve and yet there was very little communication to exactly what this was or how, in fact, each could contribute one to the other and to the association." (1-9-88-5-GBM)*

I could understand that communication was an issue in that past life and I knew that we each needed to communicate better in our current relationship, but I thought the same thing could be true for everyone in every relationship. However, as the Reader related how the past association was significant to the current relationship, my skepticism and doubt were swept away.

> *"We see that at the present time there is some frustration that exists in the one of the male once again. We see that the male does not see what this one does have to offer the one of the female. We see that there are ways that this one is aware of certain changes as they are occurring, but we see that this one does not cause there to be a preparation in this one's thoughts and this one's actions to be able to use the changes to this one's own benefit as well as to the benefit of the female." (1-9-88-5-GBM)*

As a single parent, I was insecure in raising Michelle. Although I was the oldest of six children and I'd had plenty of practice taking care of and being responsible for others, there was still a part of me that didn't know if I could handle being a parent. I also felt there were things that Michelle didn't need to know until it was time for me to tell her, feeling that I had to protect her from disappointment. Her hopes had crashed many times before when either a planned visit with her mother or other major events didn't work out.

One of the things that intrigued me about the significance of the reading was the description of the thoughts we each held and how they were often very similar. I have always been one to analyze a situation or experience, trying to figure out what happened, why it happened, and how I could improve or "fix it". A perfect example of this is my affinity with machines (probably from a past life). I have never been afraid to repair something that was broken, whether it was a car, a clothes dryer, or a computer. I had often been puzzled in my life because I expected that everyone thought the way I did. The insights from my reading helped me see that my tendency to analyze is an exceptional quality rather than a norm. I began to appreciate the way I think and recognized at the same time that Michelle thinks in a very similar manner. She wants to know how to figure things out for herself also.

> *"....in regards to communication, that there be the recognition that there are definite differences in ways of thinking and yet there are definite similarities. Would suggest to the one of the male to listen very closely to the one of the female both when there is direct communication and also when that one is in this one's presence. This one will be able to hear many of this one's own thoughts as they are expressed."*

As the Reader said there were different ways of thinking, I recalled an experience Michelle and I had just a few months earlier. She had put dirty dishes in the dishwasher after school one day. After I came home from work, I discovered that she had not loaded the dishwasher the way I taught her! She was wrong I thought. Although her approach was different, her method worked just fine. From this I could see the rigidity in my thinking that was being pointed out from this past association.

I also remembered several instances where I had a doubt or was puzzling over something in my mind and Michelle would ask or say essentially what I was thinking. It was like she was speaking my thoughts because my thoughts would be out in the open for me to view.

After the significance was related I was permitted to ask any questions. I wanted to know how Michelle and I could use the information in our current father-daughter relationship.

"We see that it would be beneficial to both to recognize each individual's personal responsibility to themselves and in regard to the use of the association. This would not be the responsibility that oftentimes these ones slip into, of thinking they need to control one another, but it would be that which would bring the attention to the conditions and circumstances that enable these ones to follow through on their thoughts, to be consistent in their thinking and their communication." (1-9-88-5-GBM)

This also made a great deal of sense to me. I worked many hours, attended my classes at the School of Metaphysics one night a week and served on several committees in the community. I felt like there were times when Michelle did give up the things she wanted because I had a meeting or other engagement. I often felt guilty and wanted to make up what I believed to be lost time with her. She would make deals to go to the movies; spending the night at a friend's house or having a friend sleep over. Each of us in our own ways influenced and tried to control the other to get what we wanted rather than communicating our desires and goals openly and honestly.

Several years ago, an attractive woman entered my life. Again there was an immediate attraction on both our parts. We talked easily and comfortably about children since we were both single parents, about metaphysics and our personal goals. We began a good friendship, and we both knew as she returned to her home, that there was more to this relationship.

Our relationship sky-rocketed several months later as we wrote fast and furiously, establishing a long-distance relationship that existed primarily on the telephone and in the mail. It was a great opportunity for both of us to express our thoughts and emotions. This was a different relationship for me, with a great deal of emphasis on mental and physical communication with very little physical time and contact. We decided to explore our relationship further and requested a Past Life Crossing. Because we'd each had readings of this type with other people, we knew we would receive an honest and objective perspective on our relationship. We also knew that we would gain a greater understanding of how we could aid each other in fulfilling desires and accomplishing goals. We would have the information to add on to that important third dimension of our relationship and we'd know how we could make the most of our physical and mental time together. In short, we'd know collectively what cards were on the table and how to play them.

Our Past Life Crossing revealed a significant relationship in England in the 1400's. The past relationship was significant because it related a previous relationship with mental attitudes and karmic learning opportunities paralleling our current relationship.

> *"We see for the one of the female to have been the mother of the one of the male. We see the one of the female to have been very domineering and we see that this one was very persuasive of what this one wanted. We see that oftentimes this one would attempt to manipulate the one of the son to do the things that this one wanted, for we see that the one of the son was often very stubborn and was reluctant in conforming to the rules and regulations." (5-20-90-1-SMR)*

The physical structure of the past relationship differed greatly from our present relationship as friends and lovers, but the mental and emotional perspectives were very much the same. In some respects though, the mother/son relationship co-existed within our current relationship. She was a very strong-willed and single-minded woman, willing to sacrifice or go to great lengths to accomplish her goals and desires. I counted on her for support, somewhat financially but mostly emotionally, during that time. When we talked, usually once a week, the long distance call was charged to her phone bill. There were many times, as we communicated by letter or phone, that I sought her emotional support, particularly when I was feeling sorry for myself or feeling that I could not achieve what I desired.

An issue surfaced in this reading that had been apparent in an earlier crossing with my daughter and in other readings I had requested. It pointed out a karmic lesson that I was beginning to recognize and deal with. The issue or karmic lesson that keeps appearing in my readings is the power of my influence. With limitations in my understanding of relationships with others, I often find myself trying to control another's attitude or action giving little or no consideration for their choices or desires. My learning in those situations is to recognize when I am being controlled and how I control others. This helps me to understand what my limitation is and why it exists, giving me freedom to change and grow in caring for myself and others.

I have heard people remark as they listen to a reading, "Oh no, am I still manipulating people" or "am I still doubting myself" or whatever a specific karmic issue might be for them. There are major karmic lessons to learn each lifetime, just as there are certain astrological influences that reflect throughout your life. I can't expect to have a single relationship where I complete all my karma about recognizing manipulation, and then never deal with the issue again this lifetime.

Karma is a universal, mental law. It is a magnificent tool for our awareness and enlightenment. Karma offers repeated opportunities to learn and put into practical application what we gain from our experiences. The operative force behind karma is intention. If your intention is to escape duty by having someone else do your work, like Tom Sawyer did while white washing Aunt Polly's fence, then as far as you are concerned you have unjustly taken advantage of another. The manipulation people fear or find repulsive occurs when only your best interests or selfish interests are served rather than the interests of everyone involved.

However, when your intention includes concern for another, you can use your influence productively to aid someone else. For instance, if our hero Tom intended to teach each of his helpers how to be the best fence white washers in Hannibal, Missouri, then his purposes would be just and advantageous to all involved. When you have an idea of how each person can benefit from an experience your influence is elevated.

At this point in my life, I was struggling with some major decisions about my personal growth, and the outcome of those decisions would impact the rest of my life. I felt like, once again, I'd set some goals for myself that I couldn't achieve. I was feeling very frustrated, as much with myself as blaming the world around me. I felt like I needed a refuge, a place to run away in case everything didn't work out. I viewed the relationship as a port to weather my mental and emotional storm and a place where I could hide.

"We do see however that the one of the son did have an attachment to the one of the mother and he did feel that this one needed to be of service to the mother. We see that due

to this type of obligation, the one of the son remained in the
home for a long period of time. We see however, even though
this one felt obligated, there were many areas where this one
would become very frustrated and very angry within the self,
for we see that this one felt that he was cheating the self due
to the fact that this one was not able to pursue many of this
one's own desires." (5-20-90-1-SMR)

One of the goals we wanted to accomplish with our reading was
to develop a closer relationship although we were physically separated
by hundreds of miles. We wanted to determine how we could help each
other fulfill individual and common goals. In response to this, the
reading had this to offer:

"....would suggest to these two that the importance is to have
open and honest communication, for we see that at the
present time period there is still a great deal of manipulation
that occurs between these two individuals. We see that much
of the manipulation is when each one feels vulnerable and
feels that each one needs someone. Would suggest to these
two that it is important for them to build individual strength
as well as strength together." (5-20-90-1-SMR)

Since our long distance relationship had been built over the phone and
by mail, we prided ourselves on our communication and the ability to
express ourselves honestly to each other. However, the Reader's
insistence on "open, and honest" communication did not come as a
shock to either one of us. I could recall conversations when I was feeling
vulnerable, lonely, or uncomfortable with myself, where I left those
undesirable thoughts and perceptions of myself unspoken. I sought
instead to find my self-value or self-esteem in someone else's eyes,
because through my own eyes, I didn't possess those qualities.

The Reader went on to suggest how I could use what I had
learned in the past association to build trust in myself, in my thoughts,
and practice open and honest communication.

"...it would be of importance for this one to practice courage
in this one's own self and for this one to be able to speak up
and speak this one's thoughts as this one thinks them, for we

see that very often this one's victimized identity is due to the
fact that this one does not express what this one has to say."
(5-20-90-1-SMR)

Truly open and honest communication is one of the keys to building and using any relationship. The idea of expressing thoughts openly and honestly incorporates trust in yourself, in your thoughts and their reality, and trust in the relationship. To use my association most productively, meant that it would be most productive for me to admit when I was feeling victimized or sorry for myself. It would give me the opportunity first, to admit such thoughts exist in my mind, and second, to physically hear my thoughts. With this type of honesty in communication, the relationship would also provide a place for me to gain another person's objective perspective as they presented truth to me about my own thoughts.

It is often very easy to "buy into" someone's limitations or poor image of himself, feeling sorry for them and supporting them when they are down. However, this is not the most productive approach. You can give them an honest and objective perspective to help them identify their thoughts. If they receive your honest communication, they'll have information to help them recognize why they have those thoughts. You offer insight to help them change their thoughts and self image.

The Secret of Intimacy

Physical closeness is not a prerequisite for a successful relationship. I have had relationships where I've experienced physical and emotional intimacy, but the most satisfying relationships I've had involved mental intimacy. You can be mentally intimate with someone else only to the degree that you are mentally intimate with yourself.

As you begin to recognize and acknowledge your thoughts, your doubts, fears and limitations, then you can also begin to recognize the same in your partner. This degree of mental intimacy permits you to work together to identify your individual strengths and build on them.

A married couple that lived in separate states requested a Past Life Crossing. She was a television executive and he was a senator in the neighboring state. They had decided to maintain a commuter marriage for career reasons.

In their past association, each admired and was attracted to the other. He was a Greek governor and she was his children's teacher. In the past association cited, the pursuit of their individual goals kept them from assuming a traditional relationship, so she and the children were in a household separate from his own. The Reader went on to say this was a way that the male controlled the female.

The significance for the current association is the same: stubbornness and individuality causes each to try to control the other. Their mental attention has been on what is missing from the relationship rather than how each can gain from the structure they've chosen, and how the relationship can be built and grow. The unique situation they've created with their relationship offers each much freedom in pursuing their individual goals that a traditional marriage would not. It also affords them an opportunity to develop that mental intimacy and challenges them creatively to make their physical time together productive and fulfilling.

Weren't You in Egypt, Say 800 B.C.?

Star-crossed lovers may have the mistaken belief that they were great lovers in a past life; Romeo and Juliet, Samson and Delilah, Cleopatra and Mark Antony. Such thinking leaves little room for all the ordinary couples in history, couples like Ezra Haddim Hezediah and his wife Esther around 800 B.C. in the area we know now as Palestine.

In their present incarnation Esther and Ezra are Laura and Calvin respectively. They met because they were students in the School of Metaphysics, he in Kansas City and she in Michigan. Their past life association revealed physical circumstances that were very similar to their current relationship. In both past and present associations, spiritual duty formed a significant role in the lifetime at that time and served as a strong foundation for the relationship. It was at least part of the mental attraction that drew the physical beings together.

> *"We see for these ones to have been a part of a group of people whose affiliation was religious in nature. We see for*

this to have been Hebrew. We see that the families were very close and that there were many opportunities these ones had to be in the same physical vicinity of one another.

We see for the one of the male to have been trained to tend sheep and we see for this one to have considered this a type of sacred duty. We see there to have been religious significance to this and we see that this one felt honored to accomplish this in the ways directed or expected by those in positions of authority.

We see for the one of the female to have prepared for caring for large groups of people. We see that this was primarily involving that of preparing food. We see that this one took this responsibility in a serious way. And we see that this one, although there was a desire to experiment, refrained from it because this one respected the traditions and the significance of the position this one was being trained for. We see that there was a kind of respect that these ones held in regards to their own chosen duties as well as in regards to their relationship to each other."

In the present , one way Calvin and Laura expressed a commitment to pursue their spiritual growth was by aiding others by teaching spiritual principles.

Like Laura and Calvin, each party in a relationship has expressed some degree of commitment to the relationship. The commitment is not always a spoken or written commitment, yet it exists and can take many different forms. For example, in your relationship with your employer, you have made a commitment to perform a certain type of work for a specific number of hours for financial gain, medical and vacation benefits and security. In a relationship with a sibling there may be a commitment to listen to the other's problems or concerns, share the care and responsibility of aging parents or trade babysitting services. In a love relationship there is probably a commitment to be the "one and only" or "significant other" in someone's life, "to honor, cherish, and obey in sickness and in health".

Much of this type of commitment may be expressed as contractual commitment. Some form of contract, whether written, spoken or unspoken, is the foundation for the commitment.

The most beneficial form of commitment in any relationship is the mental commitment first to your Self and your learning in the relationship, and second to the other person and their learning in the relationship. This is a very personal and intimate application of commitment. This is the type of commitment evident in Calvin's and Laura's relationship. Each desires to aid the other in becoming the very best they can be.

To begin that process in any relationship, it is important to recognize how the relationship currently exists. The significance of a Past Life Crossing pinpoints the relationship as it exists now:

"We see once again for there to be common interests between these two and we see that there is a respect that these ones hold, once again in regards to duty or position. We see that there is much that these ones are seeking in terms of what can be brought to the positions that these ones hold. We see in this way there is once again the accomplishment of the type of respect and the type of openness to experiencing in terms of how each can affect others. We see there is a kind of admiration these ones have for one another in regards to this." (9-9-90-2-BGO)

When you make a mental commitment to a relationship, you are making a commitment beyond the physical and emotional needs of the individuals to the souls that are involved in the association. The ideals or desires of the souls determine where the relationship can go. As you examine the relationship from the perspective of the soul and the learning that can occur, you can determine spiritual goals for the relationship that are in alignment with the individuals. You know where the relationship is and you begin to formulate where you individually and collectively want to go. The focus of a mental commitment to a relationship centers around personal growth and soul progression. You are investing your Self in aiding your mate to achieve their soul's desires or helping them fulfill their "mission" for this lifetime. What a marvelous gift to offer the other half in any relationship, a commitment that says, "I'm going to do whatever it takes to make the most of this relationship for my Self and for you!"

Give me a Sign!

It is exciting to imagine the possibilities of past lives you've lived and past associations you've had. Perhaps you and your father were fellow trappers exploring the Northwest Passage or discovering trade routes to the New World. Maybe you and your boyfriend were landowners in China during the Ming Dynasty or alchemists experimenting to turn lead into gold. What if you were a sheriff in the Old West and your sister was the schoolmarm or the local saloon girl?

There are physical and mental signs in any relationship to give you clues about your past associations. For instance, common interests about food, music, favorite times in history, similar tastes in books or clothes or movies can all be relevant to your past association. The best indication of the past associations is your own intuition, your "gut" feelings. A mental clue to the significance of your relationship is to determine recurrent problems or challenges. You may discover that you and the other person get frustrated because you don't feel like you communicate your ideas completely. You may determine you both repress your anger at the other or express your emotions too easily.

Laura and I requested a Past Life Crossing several months ago. We shared living quarters at a School of Metaphysics Center. Laura directed the Center and I was her teacher and supervisor. The reading would help us to live and work together more productively. It would also provide information to help me be a better teacher to Laura and aid me to know how to help her gain more control in the events and circumstances in her life as she learned how to direct the school.

The afternoon of the reading, we were voicing our thoughts about the upcoming reading. "What do you think we were?" Laura asked as we washed a few dishes. She was referring of course to the structure of our past relationship. "I think we were probably father and daughter," I suggested, very confident in the recognition of my thought. As we sat in front of the Reader and Conductor later that afternoon, we discovered Laura was my stepdaughter in Turkey in 400 A.D.

Neither one of us seem to have a particular affinity for Turkish food, at least not that we are aware of. There seems not to be a collective affinity to that particular time period, peasant garb or anything that one might associate with that lifetime. My intuition however was accurate. Since I first moved to Michigan, I felt Laura was like a daughter to me, that she had been placed in my charge for her growth and development.

You may be able to assess what a past relationship might have been or where or when, but only with objective analysis can you understand the desires of the souls involved in the relationship. The important part about the Past Life Crossings is the depth and insight they afford on using the relationship and developing it from the soul's perspective.

The purpose of the Past Life Crossings is to reveal to you a past association that is relevant, karmically speaking, to what is going on in your life and your relationship at the time of the reading. It offers significant insight and information so you can be a happier, healthier, and more productive person by applying the reading to your life and relationship.

The Reader identifies your vibration through your name when the Conductor says "You will search for the identity of the entity referred to as John David Doe". This identification would be analogous to having a negative of a photograph, your vibration, and searching through boxes of pictures, the Akashic Record, for a picture that most closely matches that negative. When the Reader responds, "We have this", the picture of John David Doe that matches the negative has been found.

As the Conductor continues, "You will search for a significant crossing of paths with this one referred to as John David Doe and that one referred to as Jane Ellen Doe, and relate a significant crossing," the Reader's inner attention is directed toward using the vibration or mental negative of Jane Ellen Doe to find an Akashic picture of John and Jane together.

There may be many of these group Akashic pictures. Some of the pictures may match the negatives of Jane and John as they exist today, some may not. School of Metaphysics readings are designed to locate the picture or past association that most closely matches the current relationship. There may be pictures of John and Jane together in the Akashic Records but none of them match the negatives. This may be because the relationship is very distant or uninvolved.

Such was the case with Mary and her four-year-old daughter Aimee. Mary was divorced and she had agreed Aimee's father would have custody. Since Mary was following her own spiritual path, she knew it would be important for her to meet the spiritual needs of her daughter as well as her physical and emotional needs. The Conductor asked the Reader to find a significant crossing for the two. After a brief pause, the Reader replied, "This is not seen."

No past relationship was found which significantly matched the current relationship. This may have been because of Aimee's young age, a transitional period in the development of the relationship, or the fact that the two souls had not previously incarned together. The Conductor knew from his own past experience the bearing and value this can have upon a current relationship. He knew information could be gained about the present association which would be timely, accurate, honest and objective. He asked, "Are there any suggestions for these two entities in the present time period?"

> "We see that in the present period of time these two have desires which are very similar. We see there are many ways in which these ones are alike and that the past understood experiences are similar. It is important for these ones to realize it is their own separate individualities that are stimulating in their friendship. We see that these two do want approval from each other and in some ways try to be too much like each other. It is important for each one to maintain their own sense of individual identity....in order for both of them to recognize their own true value as individuals and also for them to understand just because something is appreciated there is not a need to change to be like what is appreciated. That is a decision which needs to be made separately, separate from the appreciation."

This portion of the reading points out how the relationship is developing and how Aimee as a child is developing. Mary is her role model and Aimee wants to grow up to be like her mother, her physical parent. This also conveys how Aimee is adopting and assuming her mother's attitudes of wanting to please and be accepted. With this knowledge, this issue can be faced and changed, particularly on the part of Mary, so each can evolve. This will change the course of their interaction in years to come rather than remain an issue they will confront time and again through the years.

Although it does not occur often, the lack of a significant past life association between two people does give them a great deal of freedom in how they create their present relationship. When no crossing has occurred, there are no karmic issues between the two people involved. This means they are free to create the kind of relationship they desire now. When this occurs, the assessment of the current relationship becomes even more important and meaningful for the two people involved.

Sometimes no significant crossing is seen, and this will occur because there are changes taking place individually or collectively in the present relationship. It has occurred several times when one person has been questioning the desire or need for the relationship to exist. Doubt and indecision will limit access to past life information because the "negative" is blurred and out of focus so no matching picture is found in the Akashic Record. When this occurs, the objective counsel given for the present time period can aid the individuals to move beyond the stagnation or confusion in their present association. Once these issues are resolved, past lifetime associations may become available for consideration.

Mary and Aimee's crossing offered significant insight into their relationship today which can aid them throughout their life as mother and daughter. Their reading illustrates the power and influence our thoughts have on our Selves and on the people in our world, how your thoughts and attitudes as a parent are reflected in your children from birth. The time from birth to seven years of age is extremely important for the physical and mental development of a child. When a baby is born, its conscious mind is like a blank chalkboard, clean and ready to be written upon. The conscious mind is that part of mind connecting with the physical organ called the brain. It is also the part of mind that reaches for experience.

During these first years our conscious perceptions, opinions, attitudes and prejudices are formulated based on our early experiences, relationships and the thoughts and attitudes of the important people in our lives. As children, we begin imitating our parents in action, in thought, attitude, and in Self image.

Mary had been studying and applying metaphysics in her daily life, so she knew the importance of causing her thoughts and attitudes to be productive and positive. She asked what attitudes she could develop that would benefit Aimee.

"Would suggest to the parent that by setting an example by
following through with what is started is the most important.
It is also important for the child to see the parent fulfilling
her own desires. We see that by any part of this one's life,
living it to its fullest and living its principles would be being
an example to the child. We see that besides the discipline
and the follow through, there are not any other specifics in
terms of how this one should train the child."

As a single parent, I recognize thoughts I've had that I needed to give up some of my goals so I could be a better parent or so my daughter could have what she wanted. I think this is probably a universal way of thinking that we have to give up what we want, to sacrifice our desires in life to settle down and raise a family. This is an attitude of "this is what I want, but I know I can't have it".

Oftentimes this approach to life is accompanied by frustration, unhappiness, or "waiting until the kids leave home" to accomplish what you've felt like you've put off. In this instance, the Reader is telling Mary it is important for Aimee to recognize that goals are important and you can accomplish what you desire. The way for Aimee to experience that kind of success in her own life is for Mary to live that kind of success.

Mary is a nurse, working evenings. There is also the physical circumstance of living in a nearby but separate city. She was concerned about her physical absence from Aimee and sought guidance concerning this.

"We see that by establishing a way of study for the child, and
also for the communication between the parent and the child
as to the purpose of the parent's absence and also the
communication of the love and concern towards the child,
would establish the conditions that would need to be present."
(12-6-88-6-CSR)

The study that the reading spoke of was for Mary to develop a form of mental discipline that Aimee could use. The benefit for Aimee, even at her early age, would be increased ability to concentrate, a greater sense of Self worth and a more clear image of herself as "Aimee" rather than "Mary's daughter".

Communication once again is an important factor in this association. Children often blame themselves because Mommy and Daddy are divorced. They think they have erred, been a bad girl or bad boy, and feel physically and emotionally torn between the parents. This is usually the result of parental attitudes, training, and experiences projected to the child. The child reacts to the expectations of the parent. This reading stresses how communication can overcome a child's misconceptions and the resulting poor Self image.

It is important that Mary communicate the physical, emotional, and mental love she has for Aimee, demonstrating that love and concern for her when they are together. By expressing her desire to fulfill personal goals, Mary will aid herself and Aimee. Aimee will begin to formulate ideas of Self worth, accomplishment, and determination that will last her many lifetimes because Mary has given her an example to live by.

Karma: Haven't We Done This Before?

Has there ever been someone in your life that you reacted strongly to, that you couldn't stand? That reaction is a response to something that the other person represents within yourself and it may seem magnified many times. The people we bring into our lives offer us a place to reflect on ourselves, who we are and what we want to accomplish. Our outer world and its relationships are a mirror of our inner world and our relationships with ourselves. There is no such thing as a karmic boo-boo or a cosmic error. That person you're reacting to has come into your life for some reason. The two of you are together, no matter how brief the time, for your mutual experiencing.

One of my first teachers of metaphysics related the story of how her relationship with her boyfriend began. After she first heard of the School of Metaphysics, she received a call from Dermot, one of the instructors at the school, about a new class starting. When they first met, Denise knew they weren't going to get along. She described Dermot as pushy, aggressive, and a know-it-all. Denise and Dermot were very much alike. The words she used to describe Dermot also described her; she was persistent about achieving her material goals and pursued them with conviction and passion.

Dermot was a good teacher, stimulating Denise to examine herself and her thoughts. Her response was to become angry and storm out of the school after class. After some time, they requested a Past Life Crossing discovering they had been together in Germany and that Dermot had been Denise's older brother. He had teased her unmercifully and she would become angry refusing to communicate.

In a later Past Life Crossing, these two were engaged to be wed through parental arrangement. When they met for the first time however they set a mutual goal to not marry the other. They built communication, cooperation, and trust as their friendship developed and they accomplished their goal! During the months and years that followed Denise and Dermot eventually became classmates and peers. Their disharmony with each other changed to an attraction and they eventually became romantically involved. As their physical relationship evolved, their Past Life Crossings reflected a parallel evolution.

The Past Life Crossing offers suggestions about how you and the other person in a relationship can use the learning from the past in your current association. The Reader and Conductor can provide an objective third-person view of your relationship so, if you listen to the information provided and apply it in your relationship, everyone concerned will benefit. If you apply the information today, the relationship will improve tomorrow.

The Reader and Conductor teams are trained to work together. They have studied the mind and its mechanics in great depth. They have applied mental law and mental techniques of discipline on a daily basis for years. Both the Reader and Conductor are insightful and also psychic. However, the information provided by way of the readings will not relate the future of the association.

A young student and her boyfriend requested a Past Life Crossing. They were at a crossroads in their association and wanted to gain more information, and to determine if they should continue the relationship. After the significance of the reading was related, they asked what direction they should take with the relationship. The Reader suggested it was up to these two individuals to determine what they wanted to achieve individually and collectively.

When we are born, we are endowed with two gifts, our own individuality and free will. Free will is our ability to make choices and we make thousands of choices each day. We choose our thoughts and words we speak. We choose what dress to wear, whether to fix meat loaf or chicken for dinner, what route to drive to work. It may seem that some of the day-to-day decisions you make are miniscule in proportion to the decisions that relate to soul progression and growth. As thinking men and women, with the ability to analyze and reason, we can choose our learning situations and what we desire to learn. The decisions you make today will affect your tomorrow.

In any association, you can choose what your purpose or mutual learning is and choose the future for your relationship based on how you and the other person in the relationship can use the relationship productively.

When requesting a Past Life Crossing, it is a matter of courtesy and respect for the other party to ask their permission to obtain the reading. After obtaining a friend's permission for a reading, a woman was concerned because the friend did not believe in reincarnation. She thought perhaps her friend's denial would somehow affect the outcome of the reading. The Conductor assured her that the information presented would be unaffected and accurate. Just because someone doesn't know where the library is located, doesn't change the information stored in the books at the library.

A woman called to ask questions about the Past Life Crossings when I was directing the School of Metaphysics in Norman. She had heard about the readings from a friend and wanted to get a crossing with her mother. During the process of the conversation I found that the woman's mother had passed away several years earlier. As we continued the conversation I informed her that a past life relationship could possibly be found, however there would be no relevance to her current relationship since her mother was deceased. Her curiosity would have been satisfied as to who they were in a past association, where they were and what they were doing, but there would be no useful information that she could apply in her life. In short, it might have made interesting conversation at a party, but provided no real service to the woman.

We recently received a very touching letter from a man in Caracas, Venezuela requesting more information about the Past Life Crossings. His wife had picked up a brochure about the readings several years earlier when they lived in Boulder, Colorado where he was attending college. At the time, he didn't pursue his wife's interest or desire for a crossing. He wrote to say their relationship had changed. He and his wife were experiencing difficulties. "We seek your help. We are lost. Help us find our way."

Change in life, in any form, can be frightening and threatening. Oftentimes we'll do anything to maintain the status quo, but when the situation is forced we'll do something about it. We think nothing of changing the oil in a car every 3,000 miles or tuning the engine or rotating the tires so the car will continue to function. That's called proper maintenance. When it comes to other, much more significant parts of our lives, we'll bargain, ignore, and become angry to maintain a sense of balance with very little thought of "proper maintenance".

A Past Life Crossing is an excellent tool to aid the longevity of your relationship, like your car it is a vehicle requiring maintenance and diagnosis. Your relationships are vehicles for your soul growth and evolution as well as your partner's.

The Past Life Crossings are a service that is provided to the communities where Schools of Metaphysics are located and to cities where trained Reader-Conductor teams schedule visits. The information presented in the readings is to help you and those others in your life to live happier, healthier, and more productive lives. We all want to know that we've made our mark on the world, left something of importance behind, touched a few lives and made a difference in the world. The information is presented to you openly, honestly, and objectively with the best wishes for its use, and your growth and soul evolution.

A computer specialist who owns his own company, Paul Blosser has been teaching applied metaphysics since 1987. He has lectured to business and professional groups, church and single groups, about dreams, time management, goal setting, creating happiness and wealth, stress alleviation and job happiness. Paul holds a B.A. in Journalism from the University of Oklahoma, and a Respondere and Qui Docet Discit degrees from the School of Metaphysics. Now a member of the staff at SOM National Headquarters, Paul's talents are many and varied. You might find him landscaping for a garden or preparing chocolate cheesecake, constructing a building or herding cattle, writing for Thresholds Quarterly *or using hands-on healing to relieve someone's pain. Paul and his wife Pam, who also contributed an essay for this book, serve as proprietors for the Dream Valley Bed & Breakfast, a campus guesthouse for relatives and visitors. Paul is now pursuing his doctoral work in Applied Metaphysics.*

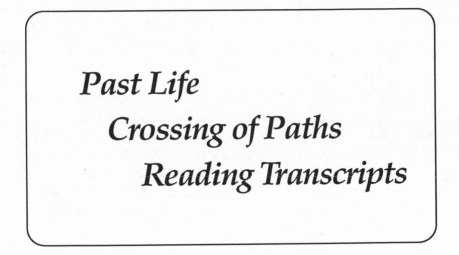

Past Life
Crossing of Paths
Reading Transcripts

B y far most of the Past Life Crossings requested are between males and females who are in love. The yearning for what many call a soulmate is strong in most of us and we desire to know everything about the object of our affections. We want our relationships to be a source of hope and joy, and with time we want them to deepen in commitment. We want to know what we can do to build a lasting association. We want to know how to weather the storms, how to grow while accepting and embracing changes in the other person. Past Life Crossings uniquely help in these pursuits for they identify the soul's purpose for the two people being together in the present.

What couples discover through Past Life Crossings is always amazing. Past Life Crossings reveal the essence of a relationship by imparting the nature of the past association. Sometimes the people discover they are indeed long separated lovers from centuries ago who have at last reunited. Sometimes they learn that in the previous life the male was female and the female, male. This is often a source of humor and at times shock or even denial. Sometimes the couple learns their previous relationship was quite different, perhaps a parent-child or business associates. Then there are the rare times – as with my high school love and me – when there is no significant crossing. Indeed, in my case, there was not any crossing seen. Ever. However, this is rare owing to thoughts and feelings of "haven't I known you before" or "it seems like we've known each other forever" that most people intuitively sense.

This first Past Life Crossing was done for a couple who were engaged to be married. It revealed that the intended marriage would not be their first.

You will search for the identify of the entity referred to as LF You will search for a significant crossing of paths with this one referred to as LF and that one referred to as JC and relate a significant crossing.

We see these ones to be in similar form. [Meaning in a body of the same sex; eg. the female in the present lifetime was also female in this past life.-Ed.] *We see these ones to be in the area referred to as Palestine. We see that these ones were part of the Hebrew people. We see they were related as what would be considered cousins. Because their families were very close there was a kind of encouragement and expectation that these two would marry and add to the family unit. This was taught to these ones and they did not question it.*

We see that there was the mating of these ones at a very young age. This was in early adolescence and we see that these ones were overshadowed for the early period of their lives by their families. They, particularly the parents of these ones, were very instrumental in the forming of their [the young couple's] *opinions and their ideas. We see that there was a very strong attachment that they had toward their lifestyle and toward their religious beliefs.*

We see this was particularly true upon the part of the one of the female. We see that this one did believe in miracles and did believe in divine intervention. This was not always popular within the group of people this one was with but we see this one had a very strong sense of faith and had had experiences which led her to believe in this. We see that this was part of what was attractive to the one of the other, and mysterious to him. We see it was later that the female began to recognize how much of an attractive power this was for the one of the male. We see it did affect their relationship as it progressed.

We see the one of the male was somewhat irresponsible in terms of this one's duties. We see this one was very serious concerning his beliefs but we see this one did not always act upon them and would often be given duties that he performed inappropriately. We see this brought disfavor upon himself and, once these ones were married, upon their family. This was continually a bone of contention between these two for the one of the female did not respect this and did not support it. It was a point of shame for her in regards to the disfavor that it brought upon the family. We see that this was particularly true after they had children and we see that the one of the female had much more vision in regards to how the actions would affect the children in the years to come, whereas the one of the male only had attention on what would happen in the immediate time period and was only concerned about that.

We see there was not much sharing that occurred between these two in regards to their attitudes. Therefore there were many opportunities to offer to one another that were not taken. Much of this was because of the conditioning they had received early in their childhood. These were self-imposed barriers in regard to what their relative roles were with one another.

We see this was a point of frustration continually for the female for she had been taught that she should not express, particularly to males, any kind of criticism or any kind of opinion. We see this one did not really believe that her opinion was less than that of males, although she had been taught this, but we see this one was still reticent to share her ideas, even with the one of the husband.

We see there was some awareness upon the part of the husband in that regard, and we see this was a point of frustration for him, for we see he felt taken from time and again for there not being the kind of association that this one would have wanted. But we see this one [of the husband] *did not take any action to create that either. Therefore, we see this one would merely place the responsibility upon the female and when she would not respond as he desired, then he would become sullen rather than to take action toward what this one desired himself. We see that this was the quality of their association throughout the duration.*

We see there were some changes in regards to the way they saw themselves as there were children produced and as they grew. There was a kind of bond that was created between these two, and a kind of familiarity and a kind of comfort they did derive from each other's presence.

We see there was much restriction that both of these ones experienced. We see for the one of the male this was self-imposed. It was of his own creating and we see that in many ways this one would sabotage his own efforts to have responsibility and freedom in amongst his peers. This one was offered many opportunities within the group of people this one resided in and we see this one was inconsistent in how these opportunities would be used. Therefore, this one often was not seen as being reliable. We see this one did, however, have a kind of charisma and a kind of attitude toward people which was open and which was very magnetic. We see that this was part of what the female respected the most about her husband.

We see the restrictions for the female were self-imposed as well, and they were centered upon the expectations of other people, particularly her parents. This one felt it was too dangerous to go out of bounds in regards to these cultural limitations.

We see the association continued in this fashion until the time of withdrawal of the one of the male. We see this was through an irresponsible act upon his part. This occurred at the age of 36. We see for that one to have been referred to as Joseph Ben Hasif. We see for the one of the female to have continued to live with her family following the withdrawal of the husband until her withdrawal at the age of 44. We see for her to have been referred to as Esther Hestian. We see this time period to be 610 B.C. This is all.

What was the manner of withdrawal for the one of the female?

Blood poisoning.

What religion were they and what scriptures did they read or study?

Hebrew. We see there was some study in the Torah by the one of the male. We see that the one of the female would merely place the self in positions to be able to be privy to information that she, by culture, should not have. This was primarily in eavesdropping.

What understandings were built by each in that time period?

We see for the one of the male there was some understanding built of this one's influence upon others and the ability for this one to bring people together. For the one of the female this centered upon the ability for this one to direct her activities and to be efficient in the use of the mental faculties as well as physical action.

Were these two teachers in that time period?

Not in a formal sense, although they did pass on to their children that which they knew.

Very well, what would be the significance of that lifetime to the present lifetime for these two entities?

We see once again for there to be a tendency toward a kind of conflict within this association that arises because of restrictions these ones have held long within themselves. We see in many cases within the present, once again, these restrictions were formed in a very early period of life and we see that it is only through this association that these are coming to the front of these one's thinking. We see there is a need for these ones to explore these issues and to recognize that there need not be the fighting against or the rebellion that is a tendency for both, toward both. There can be the recognition of a type of maturity and a type of compassion which these ones do possess in dealing with themselves.

Would suggest to these ones that there be a willingness to recognize the desires upon each one's part to both give and receive and to admit the tendencies toward taking, for we see that each one in their own way does steal from themselves the availability of the freedom in responsibility. We see although this is done in differing ways we see it is a commonality between the two and they can use one another to cause there to be a greater awareness and change in regards to these attitudes.

We see upon the part of the male once again there is a tendency for this one to be somewhat unreliable and we see this is an irritation for himself as well as the other. Would suggest this one begin to determine the purposes for which he would want to align the thinking and the actions.

We see upon the part of the one of the female that, once again, the restrictions that this one places upon the self are created within this one's own thinking. We see this one at times will lay the responsibility for these restrictions outside the self where this one then feels helpless. We see this is a way that this one does lie to the self and there is a need for this one to take full freedom and responsibility for the choices that this one has made and to recognize that there are no boundaries imposed from the outside on this one, that all boundaries are produced from within, and therefore can be altered at any time. This is all.

Are there any suggestions to improve communication between these two?

We see that there is a tendency for these ones to think for one another, not necessarily specifically, but in general terms. This is to say that they have formed concepts of one another that are very broad and they will tend to imagine responses or reactions before giving each other an opportunity to be themselves. Would suggest that both want to be themselves very much. Therefore, would suggest they be willing to extend this to each other.

They ask, "How can we cause greater mental and spiritual communion in the sexual relationship?"

We see that as the attitudes of taking are resolved there would be a change in this regard. We see each one has their own insecurities in regards to the physical action of sexual communication itself and we see until these are resolved, there will continue to be the evidence of this in their encounters. Would suggest they approach this in regards to learning rather than in regards to condemning themselves or one another.

They ask, "How can we aid each other's spiritual learning?"

This would be in remaining true to themselves.

They also ask, "How can we practice and understand intimacy?"

This would be a product of steps toward being more open and honest within themselves. We see there is a desire upon each one's part to share, and we see the restrictions that inhibit the sharing are of their own making, as has been described, therefore as these are resolved individually their interrelationship will benefit.

They ask, "Are there any suggestions for using this association to understand love?"

We see there are many opportunities for this and we see these ones are becoming aware of these. We see that there is the availability for these ones to experience and to understand their own ability for love, both in its unconditional and in its conditional forms.

Any suggestions for the one of [LF] to develop greater security when she doubts [JC's] desire for her? She asks, "What is the cause for this?"

Would suggest to this one that the restrictions this one places upon the self do tend to manifest themselves as this one being reserved in expression. We see this is much of the difficulty in regards to this query. We see this one needs to express the self as this one desires, and as this occurs there will be much less attachment to how it is received by the other or what the other thinks. We see that this one's difficulty in this regard is a restriction this one places upon the self, not a doubting of the other's intentions. (1-7-92-3-BGO)

The female requesting this Past Life Crossing talks about it in this way, "We received this crossing about two years prior to getting married (this lifetime). We had decided to marry before receiving the reading. It was no surprise to either of us that we had been married before, and the description of our previous lifetime made sense: *'we see there was a kind of bond that was created between these two and a kind of familiarity and a kind of comfort they did derive from each other's presence.'* In this lifetime we liked each other when we first met and became friends long before we developed a romantic relationship. For both of us, it was very satisfying to become close friends and companions before becoming romantically involved.

"Many of the past life conditions were very different from this life. In the past, we married when young. In this lifetime we were both in our mid-30's when we met. In that lifetime we were raised in a strong religious family. In this lifetime my husband was raised in a religious family, but I was raised without any formal religion. The similarities in our attraction to each other were apparent, however. In this lifetime[JC] told me early on in our relationship that he was attracted to my commitment to ideals, as in the past he had been drawn to me because of my faith. As in the past lifetime, in this lifetime his charisma and easy-going ability to get along with all kinds of people is a great attraction for me.

"We have both used this reading to help us understand each other better. Although it has always been fairly easy for us to talk to each other about our ideals and our love for each other and our hopes and dreams, both of us had difficulty in the beginning talking about our insecurities, our fears, our angers and resentments. We have found that when we simply talk about what is on our minds, we are both very willing to listen to each other and to respond to one another's desires. It has been a continual source of discovery and oftentimes humor to discover how much we do think for each other. Thus, it has been a challenge, albeit a satisfying one, to cause ourselves to ask questions and to speak our thoughts rather than simply making decisions based on assumptions about what we think the other person wants or doesn't want.

"It has been several years now since we have had this reading, and there are still suggestions that we apply to help us improve our marriage and our Self awareness. We were both intrigued by the line in the significance that said, *'in many cases within the present ... these restrictions were formed in a very early period of life and we see it is only through this association that these are coming to the front of these ones' thinking.'* In other words, our association with each other helps us to become aware of long-standing karma. We can use our conflicts with each other for Self-counseling, to say what is on our minds and what we feel and in so doing, uncover thoughts we had buried that have kept us limited. For example, my husband has a serious disease and as a result he requires a lot of care and attention for his physical body. There are times when I feel as if there is no time or place for my needs because his are so much more immediate and obvious. Through my association with him, I often encounter these kinds of thoughts of Self-denial, and gradually I am recognizing the many ways I learned this as a young child when my father was seriously ill. The more I communicate with my husband about what I feel, the more power I experience in discovering how I have made choices based on what I was taught as a child, and how I can make different choices now. He is very open to hearing what I say and to considering my needs as long as I let him know what they are instead of assuming that he already knows.

"A primary benefit of the reading is that it has confirmed the knowledge we had: that we love each other, that we want to be ourselves, that we want to help each other to progress and mature, and that we do want to know one another at a deep and spiritual level."

As this woman describes, the greatest relevancy of the past association with her husband was in the form of attitudes toward Self, family, and life. This is common because it is the construction of thinking or attitude, not the physical circumstances, that sets karma into motion. What is always fascinating in the knowledge that comes from the readings is the fact that similar learning opportunities or spiritual lessons can be learned in very different physical environments. For these two, the small, religiously cloistered environment existing in Palestine before the birth of Jesus of Nazareth is quite different from the urban, electronically expansive environment in the present-day United States. Yet the souls' lessons for these two remain the same, whether in 600 B.C. or the 20th century.

Furthermore the lessons will remain until they are learned by each, whether in this life or another, whether together or with someone else. The idea that you are free to relieve karmic obligations with anyone is disappointing to some because they lose some of the romance. But karmic indentures exist for the enrichment of the soul, not for sensory delight. Karmic bonds are not between people, they are with the self, tying the soul to the earthly schoolroom. Once the cause or intention is understood, that understanding becomes a permanent part of the soul. Therefore those karmic bonds can be released at any time, anywhere, with anyone.

Past Life Crossings help us to understand how our relationships with others are formed and why they are important to us. We learn that our relations with others afford an unlimited possibility of experience from which we can progress and grow spiritually. This man and woman gained insight into the nature of their mutual attraction and the challenges this similarity brought with it. In the present lifetime, they chose to meet, cultivate a friendship, and develop a marriage. In the past, their souls chose the place of incarnation which led directly to the determination that they would be married to each other.

The soul's desire for learning becomes very apparent in the circumstances of birth. The conditions of incarnation are the soul's choice. Thus each soul chooses the parents, the homeland nation, the place in society, and the general probabilities for early learning, e.g. religion, schooling, etc. This universal truth has been verified time and again by the Past Life Readings, and one of the greatest ways to understand your soul's choice of parents is to have a Past Life Crossing with them. The following is a reading between a son and his father.

You will search for the identity of the entity referred to as [the Father]. You will search for a significant crossing of paths of this one referred to as [the Father] and that one referred to as [the Son] and relate that significant crossing.

We see these two in a similar form to the present. We see for this to be in Greece. We see for the one of [the Father] to be the elder brother of the one of [the Son]. We see that the one of [the Father] was seven years older. This one was very stately, very reputable and we see that this one did have many relationships with other individuals in which this one was very highly respected. We see this one's position was a type of statesman or diplomat in which this one was responsible for mediating conflicts.

We see for the one of [the Son] to admire his brother very much. We see this one did tag along with the older brother when the one of the older brother was involved in some of the negotiations. We see that the one of [the Father] did often communicate to the one of [the Son] what his way of thinking was and how he had handled the negotiations after the fact and we see this one did enjoy teaching his younger brother. We see however the one of [the Son] was very insecure and this one did not think he would ever be able to live up to what his brother was or to what his brother could accomplish. For we see the one of [the Son] did not have the same kind of charisma and did not have the same ease with people. We do see that this one was very shy, this one did keep to himself and this one did admire greatly his brother's ability to communicate and to be able to be at ease with any type of person.

We see for the one of [the Father] not to really understand the insecurity upon the part of [the Son] and this one did not even give much attention to the one of [the Son's] insecurities, but merely did share with his brother what he was doing and his ways of thinking. We see the one of [the Son] was in a kind of awe and oftentimes did not ask questions and did not communicate to his brother his own insecurities so that this one was not fully able to receive from the brother the benefit of that one's experience in being able to cause there to be a change within the self.

We see for the one of [the Father] to marry and we see that the one of [the Son] was very jealous of the attention the one of [the Father] gave to his wife and to his children when they were born. We see that [the Son] did not communicate this with his brother and that this one did continue to admire the brother for his ability to negotiate and to relate to all kinds of people.

We see this one of [the Son] did pursue his own career. We see this was making clocks. This one did enjoy the precision and the artistic creativity that went into this, but we see that this one did think that this was not nearly as important or nearly as influential nor nearly as good as the kind of stature that his brother had. We see that in the mind of the one of [the Son] this one was settling for less than what this one really

*wanted to do, which did have to do with the kind of influence this one saw
in the one of the brother. We see that once again the one of [the Father]
was really not aware of this and that this one did have his own
admiration for the skill of the one of [the Son] and that this one was
curious about his brother's occupation, but this one's main focus of
attention was on his own life and his own dealings with different kinds
of people and his own family.*

*We see for the one of [the Father] to withdraw at 64 years of age. We
see for this one to have been referred to as Nicolai Pregrove. We see for
the one of [the Son] to withdraw at 53 years of age. We see for this one
to have been referred to as Gyro Pregrove. We see for this time period
to be the 1500's.*

Very well, what would be the significance of that lifetime to the present
lifetime for these two entities?

*We see that once again there is a great amount of admiration, respect
and awe that the one of [the Son] holds for the one of [the Father]. We
see there is upon the part of [the Father] a kind of ignorance at times of
the needs and the desires of the one of [the Son]. For we see the one of
[the Father] does become very much involved with his own life and his
own interests and with his own activities. Although this one does care
very much for the one of [the Son], this one does become consumed many
times with his own ideas and his own experiences and does depend upon
communication from the one of [the Son] in order to really pay attention
to this one's needs.*

*We see upon the part of [the Son] that many times this one's insecurities
interfere with his communication with the one of [the Father]. For we
see that there is a desire upon his part to understand and to produce
within the self the kind of charisma and the kind of ease with people that
this one sees in the one of [the Father]. But when this one compares
himself with the one of [the Father] this one thinks that he falls short, and
therefore this one does back down from communicating his desire, or
asking questions or even finding out what it is that enables the one of [the
Father] to have this kind of ease in communication.*

*Would suggest to the one of [the Son] that it would benefit this one to
communicate more directly and with a greater sense of curiosity with the
one of [the Father]. Would suggest to this one that it is only his*

insecurities that keep this from occurring and that there is not any kind of disapproval upon the part of [the Father] as this one does fear. Would suggest to the one of [the Father] that it would benefit this one to communicate to the one of [the Son] the ways in which this one does depend upon the other for the other to ask questions, or for the other to reveal himself, in order for there to be a greater degree of closeness and awareness of needs. This is all.

The one of [the Father], the first vibration, has a very strong desire and will to live and he is ninety years old. The one of [the Son] asks what he can do to help him fulfill his desires?

This would be one place where it would benefit both of these ones for the one of [the Son] to ask questions. We see that because of the kind of awe that [the Son] does hold the other in, oftentimes the one of [the Son] views the other as a type of god rather than seeing this one as being a human being and as having built the kind of understandings that have been built. We see that therefore by the one of [the Son] asking questions to find out what it is that drives this other, what it is that has motivated this other, what it is that this one has built and the steps that he has taken that would provide for the one of [the Father] an opportunity to pass on what he has learned, as well as providing for the one of [the Son] the kind of knowledge that this one desires in order to build some of these qualities within the self. (3-14-93-8-LJF)

"I had known my father for nearly 35 years before we had a Past Life Crossing done. Upon hearing the reading, it made perfect sense to me why we had chosen to incarn together. For most of my life I had admired his ability to speak to anyone. I recall him saying several times, 'I never felt inferior to anyone.' He also told me many times that people are just people. My biggest lesson this lifetime has been communication. I had a big fear of speaking to people for a great many years. When I heard this reading, the light bulb definitely went off over my head. It was like saying, 'Of course!'

"My father possessed a great charisma and a great humor as well. These were traits that I began to incorporate into myself. He was very well liked for his ability to lighten the mood in a situation. I, too, have used humor in many situations to bring levity in where needed. My thought was that the universe weaves its way perfectly into our lives. I could not have thought of a more perfect match to aid me in learning this lesson of communication.

"This lifetime, especially in the last six years, I have become a teacher and director of a School of Metaphysics. It has taken a while for me to broaden my communication skills. Through lecturing, appearing on radio and TV and many other avenues, I am learning the art and skill of communication; in essence, learning to talk with anyone. My relationship with him is one which I will, of course, remember. He aided me in adding another puzzle piece in my quest for understanding."

Past Life Readings can answer questions that linger in the mind, sowing seeds of doubt, anxiety, and fear. This reading is a good example of dispelling imagined fears. All his life the son had feared that he would not find favor with his father. This reading very clearly placed the root of this fear with the son, explaining it was of his own making and disapproval was far from his father's mind. As the reading stated, *"it is only his* [the son's] *insecurities that keep this from occurring and that there is not any kind of disapproval upon the part of* [the Father] *as this one does fear."* People spend years keeping their love from the people they want most to love all because of misunderstandings such as these. Some people spend years in therapy to try to discover what can be revealed in a matter of minutes in a reading.

It was fortunate for this man that he requested a Past Life Crossing with his father *before* his father died. This information changed the way they saw one another and the way they related to one another during the father's last years. Without the reading, this would not have occurred. Also had the son waited until his father died, a Past Life Crossing would not have been possible. Because these readings are relevant to the present experience, both people must be incarned so significant information that will enhance the learning can be related. When someone is seeking insight into an association where the other person is no longer alive, I recommend questions oriented toward understanding and release upon the part of the person incarned. These types of questions can be asked in a Past Life Reading but are more appropriate in a Health Analysis. [See the final section of this book for information on this type of consultation.]

It is quite common for souls to incarn together, particularly as members of the same family unit. This is true even when the relationship to each other changes from one lifetime to another, as it did here from past life brothers to present-day father and son. The Earth supplies a rich mix of cultural attitudes that affect familial relationships. Therefore, what can be learned between two brothers about love, loyalty, authority, security, and responsibility is different from what can be learned by a father and by a son.

To experience once as a parent, another time as a spouse, another lifetime as a cousin, makes for a wide range of potential growth for the soul. It also allows for the cultivation of divine bonds of love that transcend physical time and space. Such is the case in the following reading for a husband and wife.

You will search for a significant crossing of paths with this one referred to as [Female/Wife] and that one referred to as [Male/Husband] and relate that significant crossing.

We see these two in the same form as in the present. We see for this to be in the land area referred to as Russia. We see at that time for the one of the male to be the father to the one of the female. We see that this one of the male was involved in a military position. We see this one was quite disciplined and quite gruff in this one's expression. This was due to this one's regimented ways of thinking. Because this one had placed very high expectations upon the self, these were also transferred to those of the family.

We see upon the part of the female, this one oftentimes was resentful that the one of the male seemed to be so consistent in this one's thinking and expression. We see that this one saw the other [the father] as not being willing to listen or to see her as an individual. We see there were ways this one accepted many of the rules and regulations which were part of this one's upbringing but we see that in doing so this one made many assumptions and did attempt to think for the one of the father.

We see between these ones there would be an attempt at communication, but we see the one of the father assumed that any meaningful communication the one of the female needed could go through the one of the mother. We see therefore this one of the male would oftentimes cause the self to become angered or upset when the daughter would challenge this one and would be inquisitive as to the purposes for certain actions and certain determinations.

We see that the one of the female was involved in seamstressing at that time and was quite creative in the manners in which she utilized this. We see this one was able to create a position, or a need which involved serving those ones, within the structure of the employment of the one of the father. We see this was quite unnerving to this one of the father because we see this one saw it as an invasion of this one's space and of this one's life. We see this one did not understand the needs or the expression of the one of the female, as it did not fit with this one's own assumptions. Therefore this one did not trust the self in learning how to communicate or in coping with the success and the familiarity of the one of the female to those ones that he was associated with. We see this to be primarily the way in which these two did relate and this continued throughout that time period.

We do see for the one of the female to have married . We see there were several times where this one did attempt to bridge what this one considered to be a gap in the relationship with the one of the father. We do see that in many ways the one of the female developed a great deal of rigidity in this one's thinking and did practice many of the principles that this one saw the one of the father demonstrating, as well as issuing forth in the way of directives. There were times when this one of the female would become quite angry and would fall into that same kind of behavior but we see this was the manner of expression for herself. We see for the one of the female to have withdrawn from the physical at sixty-seven. We see for the male at seventy-two. We see for the female to have been referred to as Andrea Vladadov. We see for the other Kinal Vladadov. We see for this time period; 1400.

What understandings were built by the one of the female in that time period?

We see this to involve that of discipline.

Were there any understandings built by the one of the male?

Again there was the involvement in that of discipline. There was the development of this.

What would be the significance of that lifetime to the present lifetime for these two entities?

We see at the present time there is once again a breakdown in commu-

nication. There is the idea on the part of the female that the male does not see about the self what this one wants to be seen. We see the difficulty lies in these one's ability to listen, both on the part of the female as well as the male.

We see for the male to be quite passive in this one's thinking and to be quite attached to ideas which are not always productive but which have served this one well in this one's mind. We see because of this there is the resistance to what this one might have to give up, or might have to be responsible for, if this one were to change this one's way of thinking and communication. We see each do have some difficulty in thinking for themselves when there is attention placed upon attempting to think for one another.

We see upon the part of the female that there is oftentimes a holding back and that this one will become irritated . Then [she] will communicate to a certain degree but it is not what this one is seeking to communicate. Would suggest then that this one make the time periodically to communicate exactly what this one wants to. Then cease trying to get the other one to agree or disagree but leave it rest. This would aid in these one's developing the means of forming more constructive communications and abilities – to receive one from the other. This is all. (3-2-87-2-GBM)

One of the most interesting possibilities that arise with readings involving past lives is a similarity between the past and present that explains a deja vu experience. A name holds a particular fascination and you discover this was your name or the name of a loved one in a previous life. A place seems familiar to you and you find at another time you lived there. You feel drawn to particular styles of clothing or architecture or periods of history, and a significant past life explains why. Deja vu occurred for this woman concerning the information related in this crossing, she writes:

"I am an artist. At the time I received the reading, I was involved in doing watercolor portraits for people. I always added an imaginary scene around the person whose portrait I did. I placed him or her in a situation which I thought would suit him or her the best including the right colors and costumes. My husband liked those portraits and he wanted to have one too.

"I spent some time thinking what theme would be the best for him. I had decided to make him as a king since he always playfully wanted me to call him "my majesty". I looked in magazines for an inspiration and a kingly wardrobe. There used to be an advertisement for Smirnov vodka with a Russian Czar sitting on a horse. When I saw it, I thought right away 'Yes, this is it! I will make him in a Russian uniform sitting on a horse.'

"I did the portrait as a surprise. My husband loved it and was showing the painting to everybody. A few months later I received our Past Life Crossing. He was my father and a military officer in Russia. We both were laughing when we heard it. It made sense why my husband looked so natural in the Russian uniform in my painting and why he loved it so much."

The reading also proved helpful in her relationship with her husband. Since the relationship in the present was from choice – marriage – rather than blood relation as was the case in the past, it was particularly important for the woman to heed the reading's suggestions. As occurs at times, most of these suggestions centered on one of the two people, in this case the woman, rather than the man. This most often occurs significantly. For instance, here it was the woman requesting the reading. And it was the woman who was the more sincere in understanding and using what the reading revealed.

"Our reading said that we need to learn to communicate verbally and listen to each other. I knew right away that this was right. We have telepathic communication, understanding each other's intentions, but there always was a gap in our verbal communication.

"I used to wonder why he always got so upset when I tried to give him suggestions in something he thought was his business. The reading said that he used to do it in the Russian lifetime too. He used to be upset when my business services included the people he was associated with. In the present lifetime, I thought that our relationship is more important and I stepped back in communicating what my suggestions were when I saw him upset. The suggestion to communicate periodically and leave it at rest, instead of holding back or arguing my case, helped me to be more open to him and has greatly improved our marriage."

This reading addressed the impact of a marital relationship outside of the home, in the business realm. The following Past Life Crossing was done for two people whose work brought them together. Far beyond being just a source of income, the reading illustrates the wealth of learning opportunities available for the soul in what we commonly call "the business world". Particularly noteworthy are the revelations concerning authority.

You will search for the identify of the entity referred to as [Female].

We have this.

You will search for a significant crossing of paths with this one referred to as [Female] and that one referred to as [Male] and relate that significant crossing.

We see these two in male form. We see this to be in Egypt. We see for these ones to be cousins and we see that there was a close association between them. We see that there was a great competitiveness that did arise between them. We see this did affect every area of life.

We do see that these ones were involved in a kind of athletics. We see for the one of [the Male] to be very swift and very agile. We see for the one of [the Female] to have greater endurance and strength physically. We see this was one area in which these ones did compete and did try to outdo one another. We see these ones did become very frustrated many times for we do see, although these ones were able to excel in the area that each one was proficient in, when it came to beating the other in regards to the opposite quality these ones did fail. We see that this did cause there to be many different kinds of reactions between them.

We see that there was also a competition scholastically. We see these ones did urge one another to excel as well as competing with one another. This was particularly true in regards to practicing a kind of meditation and channelling that these ones did practice. We see in this one area these ones did have in common a kind of idea that this was very sacred and very holy and that it was very important to each one that their cousin did excel. We see these ones did compete with one another [because] each one did have a basic insecurity and did think that [they] were not capable themselves of reaching the degree of closeness with spiritual forces that [they] did desire. But we see each one did think that the other was far more advanced spiritually and did therefore encourage the other to achieve in these ways, although each one did not think that they were capable themselves of accomplishing this.

We see as these ones grew older there were many different areas in which these ones did compete. We see this did occur when these ones were choosing mates. We see that there was a kind of race to see which one would find a mate first. And in regards to the different mates these ones did choose, that the ones of the mates communicated with one another. This did aid these ones in building a greater honesty and objectivity with one another for we do see that their mates did not have the same kind of competition and did not really understand the source of this. We do see however these ones did continually define ways to compete for we see this did provide a challenge for each one that did stimulate them to push themselves beyond what each one motivated themselves to do alone.

We see for this association to continue until the withdrawal of the one of [the Female]. We see that this one did fall victim to an accident due to this one's recklessness and that this did cause there to be an injury that punctured this one's lungs. We see this was when this one was 42 years of age. We see for this one to have been referred to as Jezaca.

We see upon the withdrawal of this one that the one of [the Male] was very distraught and we see that this one did become very irrational for a period of time. We see for this one [of the Male] to withdraw into the self and to be very angry. We see this was primarily due to this one's discovering, after the withdrawal of the one of [the Female], that he had not shown the love that he had to the extent that he did desire. This one was very angry that the life of the one of [the Female] was taken away so abruptly. We do see eventually this one did, to some extent, resolve this through counsel from some other individuals who were within this group of people. We see for this one to withdraw at 59 years of age. We see for this one to have been referred to as Gihowla. We see for this time period to be 800 AD.

What would be the significance of that lifetime to the present lifetime for these two entities?

We see within each one of these two, there is insecurity regarding their own worth and their own value. We see that each one does perceive value and worth in one another and we see therefore these ones do establish a kind of competition between them. We see that with this competition, it does challenge each one to reach within themselves and to excel to a greater extent than each one practices on their own.

We see that, as in the present period of time, there are times when these ones do put the self down in comparison to the other and do actually encourage one another to excel in ways that they do not encourage themselves. We see there are other times when there is a kind of tearing

down that these ones do of one another. We see this is when each one
is being insecure. Would suggest to these two that the competition can
be very productive and very beneficial, but it is very important that each
one learn how to compete within themselves.

We see it would benefit these ones to elaborate upon and to identify the
particular qualities that each one does admire and respect in the other;
for these ones to learn how to cultivate and nourish these qualities within
themselves. We see that by each one competing within themselves in
regard to how each one can excel and can improve and can add to what
has been already accomplished that this is the most productive use of the
competition. We do see that it would benefit these ones as well to respect
the challenge that each one receives from the other, for we see that it is
very stimulating and it is a source of excitement for these ones to push
against one another. We see that as long as this is done with awareness
and with purpose that this can be used very productively.

Would suggest to these ones that it would benefit them to practice a kind
of nurturing towards themselves. For we see that each in their own way
does nurture the other but that these ones do have difficulty giving this
to themselves and this is once again due to the insecurities that have been
related. This is all.

The one of [the Male], that is the second vibration, says "how can he best
aid [the Female] in her soul growth?"

Would suggest to this one it would benefit this one to be more verbal and
more openly expressive with this one's love. We do see that this one is
very loving and that this one does experience much love for the other, but
we see this one does not recognize the extent to which the other is
insecure. We see therefore this one assumes that the other will know of
this one's love due to this one's actions. But we see that by verbalizing
this, by being much more expressive emotionally, much more specific in
the communication of this, it would aid the other to know that there is love
and that this one has worth.

The one of [the Female], the first vibration, says "How can she best aid
[the Male] in his soul growth?"

Would suggest to this one to learn respect. We do see this one does desire
to give and we see there is much that this one has to offer, but we see this

one becomes passive and waits for a stimulus. We see therefore this one becomes very frustrated and very bottled-up in regards to what this one wants to offer. This one does take this out on the other by trying to control him. Would suggest to this one that there is a difference in aiding and in respecting another and by this one learning [how to] respect this would aid.

Would a greater understanding of authority on the part of the one of [the Male] aid in building this relationship?

Yes. Would suggest to this one there is a difference between the use of authority and being bossy. We see each of these ones do have insecurities as have been related in regards to their own authority. Therefore these ones do tend at times, when they are being insecure, to try to boss one another rather than simply operating from what each one knows. Would suggest to each one to identify what this one does know and to operate from the security that comes from relying upon what this one does know. For we do see there is much that this one [of the male] has practiced and built and does understand, and when this one operates from this place there is security. (10-25-92-4-LJF)

These individuals sought this reading for a definite purpose and, as they describe, the information fulfilled that purpose and more. "This reading was given during a public reading session in Indianapolis, Indiana. Those present who knew us chuckled as did we when the issue of competition was raised. It was important to both of us that we learn to develop our association to its greatest potential. This stimulated the desire to obtain a Past Life Crossing.

"Probably the greatest learning I [the female] received from this reading was the knowledge of the depth of my insecurity. Before receiving this information it had never occurred to me that I was insecure. As I looked more deeply into my thoughts and motivation in this association I began to see the truth of what had been presented. Because I was so insecure, this relationship was rapidly disintegrating.

"I was actively destroying that which I desired because I was afraid I would lose it. Doesn't really make sense does it? Well, it did to me. Because I was insecure I felt the need to be in control, just as the reading described. The only way I knew how to do this was to actively create what I already feared, thus I was in control. Now, thanks to this reading I am learning to create my desires rather than my fears."

These two people no longer work directly with each other as was the case when they received this reading. Yet the learning gained through their association has benefited their relationships with others. This is true for anyone, what we understand affects our outlook on life, our choices, and our relations with others. Whatever growth is gained in today's circumstances enhances the quality of our life tomorrow. Because this is true, the information revealed in these readings, even though intimately relevant to those requesting them, is of great value to us all.

Not everyone reacts to fear, as the woman in this reading, by trying to dominate someone else but whenever fear is allowed to fester and grow it actively destroys confidence and security in its host. As revealed in this reading, fear is allowed to exist where respect is missing: *"...it would benefit these ones as well to respect the challenge that each one receives from the other, for we see that it is very stimulating and it is a source of excitement for these ones to push against one another."* It would appear this is an understanding these two people are trying to attain. They state, "As far as the competition, we still have fun with it but have learned much about motivating ourselves to be the best we can be. We actively practice beating our own personal records and encouraging the other to do the same. Okay, okay, so sometimes we still compare scores – we're learning."

Perhaps someday they will remember and bring forth the concern and support they displayed for one another in Egypt so long ago: *"....these ones did have in common a kind of idea that this was very sacred and very holy and that it was very important to each one that their cousin did excel."* Then they can be willing to aid the other toward greatness, and in so doing achieve their own, thereby excelling beyond what they were able to accomplish in the previous lifetime association: *"we see each one did think that the other was far more advanced spiritually and did therefore encourage the other to achieve in these ways, although each one did not think that they were capable themselves of accomplishing this."*

Perhaps the greatest value for anyone of this particular reading rests in the insights regarding authority. Consider these truths in your own life: *"there is a difference between the use of authority and being bossy.... Would suggest to each one to identify what this one does know and to operate from the security that comes from relying upon what this one does know.....there is much that this one has practiced and built and does understand, and when this one operates from this place there is security."*

How different the world will be when we can all understand and demonstrate these simple truths in our dealings with others.

This universality of Truth has come forth from these readings for a quarter of a century. The conductors and readers change, the Truth remains constant. The relationships of those requesting readings change – parent and child, husband and wife, employer and employee, friends, lovers, rivals, or enemies – but the Truth feeds the soul. That is the Truth that sets us free to do the work of the soul.

Part III

Family Readings

"The family is the association established by nature for the supply of man's everyday wants."

—*Aristotle (4th c B.C.)*

F amily is the incarned soul's first place of experience. The composition, kind, and quality of those childhood experiences are the foundation for the forming conscious mind.

Our research into past lives and their impact upon today shows that the soul does not carry misunderstandings. Thus fears, doubts, insecurities, prejudices, resentments, hatreds, and all other forms of limitation are not an innate part of the Self. When they exist, these are learned anew each lifetime.

The unique combination of understandings within each soul is the reason why siblings can be so very different. Situations that are fearful to one are a challenge to another; conditions adored by one are avoided by the other and so forth. One sibling repeatedly practices playing a musical instrument with mediocre progress while another demonstrates the startling ability for hearing a piece and reproducing it on command. One can remember and manage a series of numbers in mathematical sequence while another finds adding a column of figures a challenge.

How each soul's uniqueness manifests itself serves as the stimulus for family interaction. Are successes met with encouragement and shared pride, or anger and jealous rivalry? Do the actions of the parents support the principles they teach or do they sabotage every effort? Is communication open, strong, and meaningful or superficial, mandatory, and alienating? How we interact with our own family members, what we build, or destroy, with them, is reflected in all other relationships we experience during our lives. By understanding our familial relationships we deepen Self awareness and enrich every relationship we presently enjoy.

The nature of the soul's uniqueness, both in understandings and the need for them, determines the choice of birth. Once this is understood, the long-standing manipulative adage "I didn't ask to be born!" thrown by an angry and petulant child, no longer holds power over an unwitting parent. The enlightened parent understands the child's soul did indeed choose this familial environment for very specific reasons. Identifying and understanding those reasons is not only the child's responsibility in life but the parent's challenge as well, and this is where a Family Reading is most helpful for all family members.

A Family Reading seeks an incarnation where up to five family members were in association. This is the largest number of people that can be traced for previous association that will be significant. Our research has shown that more than five tend to separate, in other words five may be found in association but not the sixth, or four are identified but not the remaining three. In almost every case an association of up to five current family members has been found and described. Sometimes one or two of the family members may appear in the past life as an acquaintance or may have died before having much association with the others. When this is the case, the lifetime related tends to be more significant for those who were in closer relation in the past life and less so for the more distant individual. This is somewhat illustrated in the "Gentle women" reading related in this section; four of the women are close in association during the past life while the fifth is separated by position in society. Each family is different, and so this is also true in what is revealed in the past life associations.

In terms of past life research and insight, Family Readings are particularly interesting because there are so many dynamics involved. There is the group karma or common subconscious reason why this particular group of souls is together. Just knowing this can radically change for the better how the family relates to one another. It can also lessen any tendency to blame each other for shortcomings, and shed light on why certain situations may have arisen in the past. Knowing the karma you have in common with family members can deepen bonds of love and understanding as suggestions are acted upon.

The Family Reading also reveals how the individuals interact with one another. In one way this is demonstrated by the previous relationship and its comparison with the present relationship. For instance the mother and father in the present may have been a daughter and mother in the previous life as is the case with the other Family Reading included here. Sometimes just being aware of which significant previous relationships existed can answer questions of love, affinity, loyalty, closeness, or distrust, rejection, indifference, hostility.

For instance, a father and daughter in the present life who were husband and wife in a previous life at best experience bonds of love and at worst could be fodder for confusing sexual attractions. Knowing about the past association can help place the current relationship in a more proper perspective, freeing the self from unnecessary fear or guilt, and enabling the people to fully relate to one another through the roles they have chosen in the present. Family Readings may not cure dysfunctional families but they do shed light upon the cause for problems while giving helpful suggestions to all involved.

As Aristotle noted, *"The family is the association established by nature for the supply of man's everyday wants."* Family Readings help the members to understand their own wants as well as those of each other. And for this reason they are profoundly relevant.

Family Readings
by Daniel R. Condron, D.M., M.S.

Choices of the Soul

Have you ever asked yourself, "Why was I born in this family, with these parents and older brothers or sisters?" Have you ever wondered, why did *I choose* this family to be born into or why did I *choose* my mother and father for this lifetime?

"But," you exclaim, "I did not choose my parents. I didn't choose the time period, day, month, and year I was born. Nor did I choose my place of birth. Neither did I choose whether I would be male or female this lifetime!"

Oh, yes, a part of you did choose. Each individual is endowed with free will and has this free will whether in the physical level of consciousness or not, whether before or after a lifetime.

I was born into a family with two older siblings. In addition to these two older sisters, I have a younger brother and a younger sister. For many years I questioned why I was born into this situation. Why did I choose a farm family in which there were many aunts and uncles, grandparents and cousins from both sides of the family living in close proximity? Why did I choose to be born the same year that the double helix structure of DNA was discovered? Why did I choose to be born in 1953, a year in which there was a conjunction of Saturn and Neptune which only occurs every 144 years? These are the kinds of questions that deserve an answer and I believe everyone has the right to have the answers to these and other questions about themselves, their choices and the meaning of life.

The Family Reading developed by the School of Metaphysics provides insights into many questions the individual may have about Self, his upbringing, relationships with family in the present and the source of many present day difficulties and affinities. Did you ever ask your Self, why did dad always seem to like my brother more than me or why was mother always so strict with me but not with my sister? Or perhaps your father or mother seemed to favor you over your brothers or sisters. By investigating a past lifetime in which the family members were together, the origin of present day relationships and attitudes within the family can become more understandable.

The nature of past life associations and their impact on present experiences is increased when you can accept that you exist beyond your physical body. The physical body is a vehicle that you, the soul or spirit, use each lifetime. Between lifetimes, you exist in the soul body or vehicle of the subconscious mind existence while assimilating the previous life's experiences and preparing for the next lifetime. Therefore, each lifetime is to be used to build greater wisdom, learning and understanding within the individual. After many lifetimes of learning the Self achieves full enlightenment sometimes referred to as the Christhood. Having learned all the lessons the physical has to offer the individual need not reincarn into the physical existence but rather progresses on to a higher plane or level of existence.

Throughout your lifetimes you have been associated with many, many people. Many of these individuals you have had close associations with in the past, both pleasant and unpleasant. The choice to incarn into a specific family this lifetime relates to the experiences the soul has had with members of this family in past lifetimes, although the exact relationship in the past may be different from the current familial relationship.

A Family Reading is a very special type of Past Life Reading for this reading presents to the current family a previous lifetime in which they were associated. The Family Reading can include up to five people in an immediate family. It investigates the association of these people in a significant past lifetime period. Through research we have found the probabilities of up to five individuals sharing the same previous lifetime experiences remain high. When more individuals are added the probabilities of common past life experience with all members diminishes considerably.

Many times people desire this information to improve their present family life. For example, a husband and wife who have three children may desire to understand this relationship better in order to be more effective parents. A Family Reading will provide these parents with valuable information about themselves and effective changes they can make for their own betterment and the improvement of the family life.

At times a family may request this type of reading and want to include a grandparent in the reading. This is possible as long as the number of people in the reading does not exceed five. The closer the kinship in the present, then the more likely a time period in the past when these five were together exists because of the group karma those individuals need to complete. The more distant the kinship in the present time, the less likely all five have been together in the same time period of a lifetime prior to the present one. Learning that was begun with these individuals in a past lifetime can be enhanced and added to in the present time period through association with these same entities.

In the present life we may have a father, a mother, a daughter, and two sons. In the past life, it may be that the present-day daughter was the past-life mother and one of the sons may have been the father while the present-day father and mother may have been the children in the past lifetime. Or the parents of this lifetime may have been grandparents of that past lifetime, or perhaps cousins. To someone not acquainted with the people receiving the reading, it can be confusing to follow the different relationships of the past. But to those involved, the previous relationships answer many questions and shed light on present-day harmonies and disharmonies. This is why we always provide an audio cassette of the Family Reading. By listening to the recording of the reading many times, much more of the information is assimilated and can be applied individually and collectively.

One Family Reading included Jason, the son; Joseph, the father; Ethlyn, the mother; and Melissa, the daughter. Their past life relationships proved to be very different from their present life:

> *"We see for these ones to be within the area referred to as China. We see for these ones to have come together when a marriage was arranged between the one referred to presently as Jason and the one presently referred to as Joseph. We see that the one referred to presently as William Joseph was in female form at that time. We see the female to have entered into the household of the husband, the one presently referred to as Jason, and we see for there to have been conflict immediately between the one presently referred to as Wil-*

*liam and the one presently referred to as Melissa. We see for
the one presently referred to as Melissa to have been the
sister of the one presently referred to as Jason. We see for
these two women to have clashed and we see for them to have
experienced jealousies and envies in their physical situation.*

*We see that the one presently referred to as Melissa did not
believe that she would marry. We see that there had been
several attempts to arrange this but there had been something that would occur, whether it would be the death of the
intended spouse or some other offer that would be made to
the intended spouse that would be better or would be taken,
and this left her without a mate. We see that this had
occurred several times, and that she had begun to believe
that she would never marry. We see therefore that she did
not want her siblings to marry either, particularly this
brother because she was very attached to him and was very
fond of him and did want to control his life.*

*We see that in many ways she did view the one presently
referred to as Jason as a substitute for the husband she did
not have. We see that there was not any overt physical
affection between them or sexual involvement but we see that
in her mind she did rely upon the one presently referred to
as Jason for protection and for many of the securities that
she would have expected from a husband. Therefore when
the wife was brought into the household she very much
resented this and we see that she did try to undermine the
marriage. We see that the one presently referred to as
William, the wife, was very meek and was introverted.
Therefore it took her a while to realize the amount of
animosity that was being directed toward her."*

This reading continues describing the interaction between these three
family members. The fourth family member, the present-day mother
Ethlyn, enters the group association as the child of the couple described:

*"We see that the child was female and that this again added
another element to the dynamics of the relationship between
all of these ones, for it was another female force which as she*

grew older learned the jealousies and the introversion of the
two primary females in her life, and we see that in effect it
was the female child who began to gain all the attention of
the male." (10-6-92-1-BGC)

The family dynamics of the past life, even though different from the present, still impact the familial relations of today. As the past life portion of the reading continues, the interactions between the four are described in detail and the significance to the present lifetime is related. In the present life the son and mother continue their tendency toward siding with one another as do the father and daughter, often facing reactions of jealousy once again.

In all Family Readings given, by using the names of people of the immediate family we have been able to locate a significant association in a past time period when all five were associated in some way. In fact, very rarely is the association of the five in the past life the exact same in regards to the blood relationship as it is in the present time period for the soul has many different lessons to learn in evolving toward enlightenment.

The Soul's Lineage

Each lifetime provides a different set of situations and circumstances, a different "classroom" in which to learn and grow. In school, you may take a course in chemistry, another in languages, and still another in history. Many different courses are required in order to learn the lessons necessary to graduate from high school and earn a diploma. Similarly, through many lifetimes the soul incarns into different environments, sometimes in a female body, other lifetimes in a male body. Between lifetimes the soul exists in subconscious mind for the subconscious mind is the abode of the soul. The soul will incarn in one race, and the next lifetime in a body of a different race. Each of us in our soul travels have incarned in many places on this earth, from Europe to Africa to Asia to North and South America.

Each individual has a unique purpose. It is the duty and responsibility of each individual within that family to discover their purpose for choosing that particular family in order that they may use the association to the fullest. Insight into these purposes is revealed in the significance of the past life association to the present life. This is illustrated from the reading cited earlier in this way:

> *"We see once again for the commonality between these ones to be in how they are motivated. We see that once again there is a need for external motivation for all of them to be able to move forward in their thinking. We see that they are often prone to falling into rash decisions or opinions which actually do not have much of a foundation, and we see that in doing so these ones rely upon each other for support of their opinions or belief.*
>
> *We see that many times, as was in the past, this is not in a productive sense to find courage in confidence in being able to reproduce but rather it is in being able to justify their limitations...*
>
> *We see that there is a great sense of connection that these ones have, there is a very real sense of bonding that these ones have, and we see that no matter what disagreements they may entertain or what kinds of conflicts arise, it does not hinder the bond. We see however that there is an attempt upon these ones part, once again, to expect a kind of magical revelation from the bond in producing understanding. As was in the past this did not occur, and it does not occur in the present.*
>
> *We see there is some need on each one of these one's parts to recognize that understanding is the result of individual desire and effort, it is not something that occurs merely because situations force the self into understanding. We see that each one of these ones are capable of much greater understanding than they give themselves credit for in the present time period..." (10-6-92-1-BGC)*

This reading goes on to give suggestions for change to the family as a group as well as offering specific insights for each of the four family members. Jason is encouraged to face what is unpleasant rather than becoming distant and backing away when conflicts arise by creating a fuller realization of responsibility for Self and his life. William's tendency toward vacillating between stubbornness and indecisiveness is noted as a root for personal and family frustration. Suggestions for contemplation and reflection on ideals and purposes are given. Melissa is described as dynamic and aggressive, having powerful influence in the family. Her short-sightedness and narrowness of vision causes her to discount this, thus becoming irresponsible. She is encouraged to extend her thinking into the future to realize her influence over a prolonged period of time. Ethlyn's attachment to people causes her to change loyalties easily, leaving her dependent and needy. Ways of developing confidence in weak areas are outlined to aid in her individual growth and progression. When put into practice, the specific suggestions for the individual family members will improve not only their relationships with each other but with others in their lives.

Within an immediate family, there needs to be a variety of different associations so that individuals can experience different kinds of learning. The father in this lifetime may be practicing authority while the son is developing trust, follow through, and discipline. Some of the types of understanding or permanent learning that a person can develop in a lifetime are: discipline, pride, authority, love, value, respect, follow through, will power, receptivity, reasoning, intuition, determination, perception, communication, power, commitment, and Self motivation.

A Family Reading provides a case history of that particular family. The significant events of the past lifetime many times parallel events of the present association in the way that people act, react, and respond to each other's desires. You might consider this to be the soul's lineage, its roots so to speak. For just as an individual may investigate his family tree, discovering his physical ancestors, so he may also desire to know the history of his soul and the other souls he has associated with throughout history.

Our individual karmic obligations become apparent as we interact with others, and family units often reveal commonalities in the need for understanding certain qualities. These commonalities can be described as group karma. Group karma is often addressed in the section of the reading called the significance. This part of the reading shows how the past lifetime is relative to the present. One family discovered how to more effectively use their emotions in order to deepen communication:

"In regards to emotional issues that have already been described, there has been a tendency within this group for there to be a siding. We see that it comes in a variety of forms and combinations. There is no one that is more prominent than another and this was true within the past lifetime related as well. This tendency to look for support does cause there to be a division within this unit. It does cause there to be misperceptions and misconceptions upon each of the individual's parts. Would suggest that these ones cease to take hearsay about what another has said or done and begin to communicate more directly with one another. This would be of great benefit in causing there to be the unraveling of some of the emotional disruptions that occur in this group and it would aid these ones to be more open and honest with themselves in being willing to if necessary confront one another with ideas, opinions, issues, that have not been resolved. Would suggest to these ones there is no excuse for these not being resolved for we see each one of these ones to be intelligent and we do find for each one of these ones to have a concern and caring for one another. Would suggest that this be where the attention is focused and that the communication come from this place." (5-25-91-3-BGO)

Another reading identified the need to learn to listen as the group karma experienced in the family. It aptly describes the individual karmic indentures, how they are similar in each family member and how they can use their relationships with each other to gain permanent understanding.

"We see that there is a need for all of these ones to build their listening capacity for we see that for the most part they all can be very vocal in expressing themselves, but we see that their listening capacity is not equal to their ability to express. It would be of benefit to all individually and collectively for the listening skills to be built for this would enrich their individual communication whether between one or two of them or all of them. It would also alleviate many temporary misunderstandings that do occur in their association.

We see that there are many aspects to these associations in

terms of how they impact one another; in terms of depend-
ability, reliability, and dependence. These are basic issues
that these ones are confronting within the associations.
Would suggest that these ones keep these in mind when there
are dealings (with each other) and attempt to remain as
open and as honest about themselves as they can in regards
to whether their sense of individuality is being lost because
of dependency or if there needs to be listening or expression
or if there is a tendency toward talking to one of the other
people rather than talking directly to the person that they
need to talk with." (12-14-91-15-BGO)

Sometimes the karmic similarities are less pronounced, particularly when one or two members of the present family were more
distant relatives or merely family acquaintances in the past. In one
reading, we find one member of the present family was not a member
of the family in the past lifetime related. This individual was, however,
associated with the others. Two of these attended school together in
their later school years, and they established a friendship based upon
their academic interest. In later years they worked together to bring
about academic reforms developing scholarship programs as well as
incorporating practical study in a program that previously had been
mainly theoretical. Roles can change in various lifetimes, yet we have
chosen to be with the people that are close to us today in order to continue
the learning that may have begun many lifetimes ago.

In addition to information concerning the relationship of the
five to each other, the Family Reading can provide information about
the land area or country in which this association took place, the time
period and the occupations of the family members. Consider these
excerpts from a Family Reading dating back to 340 B.C. in Peru:

"We see for these ones to have been what is referred to as
Inca (or pre-Inca). We see for the one presently referred to
as Anna to have been the daughter of the one presently
referred to as Charles. We see for the one presently referred
to as Charles to have been in female form and we see for that
one to have been partnered with the one presently referred
to as Tonya, who was in male form. We see for their
association to have been one of necessity. We see that the

marriage had been arranged and had not been from choice and we see for the one presently referred to as Tonya to have resisted this. We see that there were very definite ideas that this one held of what this one wanted to accomplish and what this one wanted to do with the life and did not at the time of being married have anything to do with marriage. We see however for there to have been much pressure that was placed on that one to move in that direction and we see that because this one wanted to attain certain positions within this group of people this one did accept this...

We see that the one of the child, the one presently referred to as Anna, did have much of the mother's attention and we see that the one of the husband paid very little attention to the child until she began to exhibit types of intuitive visions. We see that this did gain the attention of the father and we see that it was at that time that the one presently referred to as Debora did become involved more directly with this family unit.

We see for the one presently referred to as Debora to have been in female form and to have been the daughter of what would be termed the shaman within this particular group of people. We see that because she was the daughter of that individual this one had much information and was privy to much knowledge in regard to the duties and functions and abilities of the shaman and we see that there was a closeness that developed between that one and the one presently referred to as Tonya, the husband....we see although there was a closeness between these two and a kind of friendship which was not commonplace in this group of people, it was very natural for the one presently referred to as Debora and there was no questioning it. ...

We see the one of the male did bring the daughter to the one presently referred to as Debora and this was for a kind of evaluation. We see that the intention upon the part of the father was to gain some training for his daughter from the shaman. We see that it was through a variety of what could be termed tests that the one of the daughter did prove herself and we see that this was when the one presently referred to

as Debora did serve as a communicator to the shaman of this
young girl's abilities. We see that many of her abilities were
in regards to a kind of healing...."(5-25-91-3-BGO)

This reading continues to describe the past associations incorporating two more family members and revealing more information about the Inca way of life during that time period. At one point it states that these people were invested in the Inca way of life, holding a great respect for tradition and ancestry. The information given concerning the land area, people and their culture is fascinating, but the true value of the past revealed in Family Readings remains in the relationships of those involved. In each crossing, the major attitudes and activities of the family members are revealed and the historical accounts appear as they are relevant to those activities.

Common Dreams, Individual Learning

In each Family Reading the relationship and significance of the past life association to the present life family is given. This section of the reading, called the "significance to the present lifetime", offers a wealth of information about how to improve the relationship among the people requesting the reading. It also offers valuable insight into how each member of the family can improve themselves. Topics covered vary from communication to discipline, from pride to love, from concentration to Self value.

A variety of troubling attitudes can also be identified. Guilt, doubt, fear, condemnation, anger, hatred, resentment or need for purpose in the relationships will be described when appropriate to the individuals requesting a Family Reading. The present-day significance for the family previously associated in Peru began by identifying the ways of thinking they have in common. It continues on to describe how each family member relates to the others:

"We see within the present period, there are very definite
attitudes that hold these ones together and that are shared.
We see that these also cause the points of conflict. We see
that each one of these ones are very unique individuals with
varying degrees of strength in the personalities. We see that

> *these are very similar to the past lifetime related.*
>
> *We see within the present the one of Tonya to be the strongest of the members within this family and we see that the one of Debora also displays very definite attitudes and very definite strengths. We see that the influence these ones do impact upon one another and upon the remaining family members cause a kind of influence and repercussion in terms of the way that they think and the way they communicate. Once again the initiator much of the time is the one presently referred to as Tonya and we see that there is a kind of responsibility this one does take for causing the climate of this family to be as it is. We see this one often feels responsible for the attitudes and moods of other people even though this one will not take action upon it, whereas the one presently referred to as Debora does take action upon it. We see once again for her to often be in a kind of counselor role. It is often this one who does hear the opinions, ideas, or difficulties of the ones of the others particularly the ones of Anna and Avram. We see that once again those two do look at life in very physical terms and we see they become very opinionated as a result of it. We see that there is a kind of limiting of vision that occurs within those two as well as the one presently referred to as Charles. We see the one of Charles however to become much more stubborn in this one's attitudes than the ones of the other two. We see therefore for there to be more communication between all of these ones except the one of Charles."*

The reading continues to elaborate on the specific attitudes held by each family member: Charles' isolation and egotism, Debora's irritation and need for love, Tonya's frustration in trying to control the lives of the others, Anna's sense of failure, and Avram's selfishness. It offers suggestions for personal change to each family member, then gives the following suggestion to the family as a whole:

> *"We see once again there are psychic abilities, particularly upon the part of the one presently referred to as Debora, and we see that there is much that could be developed in this regard as well for we see all of these ones take for granted*

much of the communication that goes on between them which is telepathic in nature. Would suggest that these ones begin to examine this. We see that these ones impact one another very strongly emotionally and there are very strong emotional bonds between these ones. It would be of benefit for these ones to learn how to separate the emotions from their own patterns of thinking. We see that there are similarities in the ways these ones think but there are very individual ways also and for the health of each individual concerned it would be of benefit for these ones to independently examine this and to begin to separate their own thoughts and emotions from that of each other so there could be more insight and control of the selves and therefore more of a recognition of their own sense of identity." (5-25-91-3-BGO)

This family is a close-knit unit in the present lifetime, frequently interacting. The choice for consistent interaction affords them frequent opportunities for Self examination and growth through using the family ties. As time passes, some families drift apart. Separated by physical distance, opportunities for interaction decrease. The following reading addresses this, offering a way to strengthen familial relationships:

"We see within the present period of time that because of the goals of each, as well as the lack of attention, these five do not really come together. We see that it would benefit these ones to establish some kind of common goal and purpose for their relationships with each other to center around."

The reading elaborated on this point later, when a family member asked for more information concerning the common dream these ones share.

"Each one secretly fantasizes about how people would relate with each other in an ideal way. Each one has an idea of what they think the ultimate achievement for an individual is in terms of what mankind is reaching for and as to what they as individuals are reaching for or to become. We see that each one also does have some images that they normally keep fairly secret from each other in terms of their beliefs about life, death, the purpose of life. Some of them share with

> *other people slightly but for the most part, each one of these*
> *ones as individuals keep all of these ideas and things which*
> *comprise their dream of what they would like to be to*
> *themselves. Therefore there is not the ability to work*
> *together as a group to achieve it. We see that a few of them*
> *have found other individuals who think along some of the*
> *same lines that they share some with but there could be much*
> *more learning within the family as well as outside of the*
> *family if they would start speaking these things. Their*
> *dreams would also become more clear in their conscious*
> *mind and realization if they spoke out loud these things*
> *which they hold secret in regards to this dream now." (1-9-*
> *87-1-CSR)*

By using this part of the significance given in the reading, this family is more aware of the need to set family goals. In a productive association there need to be common goals. These goals give the members of the family a common direction in which to move the family. For example, growing up on a Midwestern farm provided me a family with a common goal of raising crops and livestock. I had regular chores about the farm such as feeding the hogs and cattle and milking the cows. In addition, during the summer I helped my father plant corn and soybeans. I and my brother also worked with our father to cut hay and put it in the barn for storing until the following winter. My mother and sisters sometimes aided with the equipment and livestock. They worked in the garden growing foods to be eaten or canned and stored for the winter. So you see, we worked together as a team towards the goal of producing food, shelter, and clothing for our family. This working together process created a closeness among all of us that continues to this day. There is the need to communicate the hopes, desires, and aspirations of one to the other so that family members are aware not only of the source of their differences but also of the common bonds that keep a family together.

Another Family Reading brings out the need for common learning in the family, explaining the relationship of individual growth to familial learning opportunities. The reading reveals the cause of family members feeling isolated or apart from each other. Until each family member recognizes his or her part, the family remains distant parts of a whole and cooperation is absent. The main focus in this reading is for the family to identify the learning that is available through this group both individually and as a whole. The qualities of cooperation and communication need to be developed here as well as common goals and purposes. By communicating, these individuals become a family in more than name only, working together to accomplish goals.

In some Family Readings the significance begins by presenting suggestions to one member rather than the group as a whole. The following reading identifies the key person in the family. In the present day Robert is Terri's husband, Virginia is Robert's mother, Carol his sister, and Beau is Terri's natural son who has been adopted by Robert.

"We see once again for these ones to impact one another in very definite and individual ways. We see that there is a kind of collective consciousness which revolves around the one referred to as Robert. We see that in many ways that one is the connecting link between all the others. We see that therefore there is much that can be learned in terms of the relative positions of the male and female in regards to their association.

We see once again there is a tendency upon the part of the one of Robert to be somewhat retired in this one's abilities to deal with emotional issues. We see once again there is awareness that these need to be responded to, and there is the willingness upon this one's part to make conditions as such that they can be dealt with. This one does tend to postpone his own development in that way. We see that this is encouraged by the ones of Virginia and Carol, this postponement, but the coming to terms with this is encouraged by the one of Terri. Therefore there is a kind of jealousy that occurs between the ones of Virginia and Carol toward the one of Terri. We see that there is some feeling upon the part of Virginia and Carol that they cannot offer the one of Robert what the one of Terri can. Would suggest to those ones in that regard that this is true and that it does not in any way reflect badly upon them. Nor does it cause there to be reason for dislike or discredit or devaluing of themselves or the one of Terri.

Would suggest however that these ones come to terms with this and recognize the value of what they as individuals have to offer. We see that this is still a significant difficulty upon the part of the ones of Virginia and Carol that they still have a tendency to devalue who they are as individuals and what they have to offer. This is much of what their learning is centered around in the present time period, once again. The one of Robert stimulates their individuality and therefore can assist them in developing this.

We see that there is also some assistance from the one referred to presently as Beau in terms of this one's ability to stimulate a kind of inner desire within all of these individuals toward that which is beyond the physical, toward that which could be termed spiritual, toward that which could be seen as new and inviting and exploratory." (12-14-91-14-BGO)

At the time of this reading Beau was just reaching school age. The power of his influence upon this family is identified as centering upon his youthful curiosity. Although the reading involves other family members, considerable information was directed toward the relationships between Robert, Terri, and Beau which has aided the smaller family unit.

The following excerpt begins by focusing on the mother of the family, Lorraine. The influence of her way of thinking is apparent in the attitudes of her children David and Connie as they approach adolescence.

"We see within the present period of time that once again the one referred to as Lorraine has a sense of jealousy towards these ones in which this one wants to have the strongest influence upon them. We see that there is a need for this one to come to terms with the more honest use of this one's own power and to release these ones in this one's own thinking to make their own decisions and go about their own way. We see for all of these ones, once again, to base most of their values around their physical gains. We see that each one will forsake and compromise principles to be able to have materially what they want, or what they see would give them the most selfishly at any given time.

We see that, once again, the ones referred to as David and

Connie do have a greater curiosity in the understanding of higher ideals; and we see for these ones many times to recognize wrong attitudes and moves upon the part of the rest of the family. We see, however, that these ones do not usually stand up for their own principles, either with their family members or in the rest of their life and will still go along with the crowd. Would suggest to these two to begin building up some strength and some bravery, to make a stand for what they do believe in and to live by what they believe in, instead of going along with others when this goes against the beliefs of these two. We see, once again, there is a communication between them that could be very good for these two. We see, however, by the communication they do have that many times they will use it to relieve some of their pressure and then not take action on what they need to take action on. We see that as a whole there is need for this family to learn a greater sense of principles and values based around the individual and the gains of the individual that are more than physical, but that would deal with a greater sense of morality and a greater sense of understood experiences and integrity."   (4-2-86-1-CSR)

It seems that everyone desires to have enjoyment, fulfillment, growth and learning in their life. To waste is a mistake for it slows learning. When nearing death, most people's regrets about their lives are for those things they have not done. When opportunities for sharing, giving and communication are passed over or avoided, the individual always gets hurt for they miss out on the learning.

Whatever the difficulty, communication can be an aid to enhance learning. Communication, however, is a two way street. It involves both talking and listening on the part of all parties concerned. Any organization, group, family, or structure of people is to be used for the individual's learning and growth for this is why we exist on the physical plane. When we can share our thoughts and activities with others of like minds our experiences on earth are more pleasant and often more rewarding. The family unit remains the cornerstone of our physical existence in one lifetime. Our early interactions with family members lay the foundation for the values we will hold, the dreams we will envision and the inner security to live those dreams. Family

Readings uncover these productive elements of association and free family members to see themselves and each other in a new light.

Mental Heredity

There is a third important facet of Family Readings. This part consists of the specific questions the family may have, both about the past lifetime related and about the present. The body of the reading is complete since it is designed to give the information most needed and useful for the soul growth of each individual in the group. Yet many have questions of a specific nature, and any question revolving around the past or present which concerns family members can be asked.

To illustrate the wealth and variety of information available through the use of a Family Reading, consider these excerpts. Each give a glimpse of the wide range of personal interest questions that are relative to the information available in this kind of reading. First, questions concerning the past lifetime association are noted, then the Reader's response:

•Do you find this family to have an understanding of the workings of mind?
"The two men did develop some understanding of reasoning and related workings of the mind."

Did any of these entities have a formal education?
"All of them did."

Do you find any of them involved in the fine arts in creative artistic abilities?
"Only in the ways described."

What seemed to be the common goal that brought this family together during that lifetime?
"Wealth was needed to be learned by each of these as it was a common desire as well."

Were there unresolved situations that were not satisfied in the family during that time?
"Only desires that were not completely fulfilled."

Some questions pertain to unified pursuits during the past lifetime association, such as the following.

•Do you find this family to have been involved in the religious activities of that time and area?
"We see for the father to have been Catholic and to have followed this fairly closely. We see that religion was something that was private to him and although the wife was born Catholic, there was not really much attention which she gave to it until the marriage."

The kind of religion followed in the past life is a common question that often aids family members in understanding their present day religious preferences or lack thereof. A family may have been Jewish in the past lifetime given and Catholic in the present lifetime. They have been Moslem or Hindu in the past and are Christian this lifetime.

People also derive insight from the identification of talents and skills demonstrated in the past life. Many times they discover these have a bearing on the present-day preferences for career choice or hobbies. They can also be a source of stimulation for latent abilities that can be brought forward and used in the present lifetime.

•Do you find any of these entities delving into painting or sculpting?
"We see for the father to be very artistic in the use of really any medium. We see for the youngest daughter to have talents as well. We see that the son was very good at drawing and was very good at designs and plans as well. He was not as skilled in painting."

The writing the mother did, was this involved in the business in any way?
"No."

Did the writing ever become published?
"There was one book that became published which was a combination of poems that this one had written."

How would this book be referred to at the present time?

> *"It is not in print at the present time. We see it referred to as Those of the Lost Soul."*

Questions can also be asked concerning the present-day relationships between family members. These often reveal the essence of strong affinities or uncover deep-seated conflicts. The responses are directed to the family members in question and often information is given concerning how these members impact the remainder of the family.

> •The one of Lyn Lou asks the question, why is there friction between herself and the one referred to as Len?
> *"We see for this to be due to some lack of receptivity where there is not a knowing of the complete facts, and we see that it is mostly stemming from incomplete communication."*

> She also asks the question, why are we not a close-knit family?
> *"Because each one has difficulty in using situations or people to learn with."*

> What karmic debt links us together as a family and how can we rise above it?
> *"It is the karmic debt of each one individually to establish their own will power to use it productively. It is also common with each individual in the family that there is a need for self-control and self-discipline. By developing these qualities and skills individually this would aid in using the family unit to a greater extent."*

> What are the individual destinies for this lifetime?
> *"Whatever these ones choose it to be."*

> What are the souls' goals for this life?
> *"The goals are to be realized and said in the conscious mind. The complete answer won't be given for this question."*

In this last question, the reason the souls' goals would not be given is the respect for the potential learning associated with causing the Self to discover the answer to this question. In readings involving past lifetimes, occasionally the person requesting the reading will ask a question which is not directly answered. When this occurs, however, the reply will revolve around potential actions the querent can pursue to reveal the answer to Self.

Many questions center on suggestions for greater familial understanding and harmony:

•Why are these ones not happy and fulfilled?
"They are to the extent they have been able to cause it."

Are there suggestions for bringing harmony into this family?
"To show more respect for each other's choices, more honest and open communication. These are the primary factors."

Are there suggestions for the one of Peter as to how to set goals and act on them?
"We see that it is the setting of goals where this one needs to learn more. We see that this one knows how to follow through or to be determined with goals when he does have one. This does not mean he always does it, but he does know how and there is a need for this effort. This is what will cause the difference in his thinking to pay off and will be something of use to him."

From these reading question and answer excerpts, you can see the large variety of information that is available. Questions that may have been troubling the family for years can be answered. The reading will show the reason these problems exist and suggestions for their relief.

One of the questions concerned the family's karmic debt to each other. Karma is defined as indebtedness as an individual. That is, the debt you owe to yourself to learn and grow to become a whole, functioning Self. A whole, functioning Self is a person who is using all parts of Self fully drawing upon present and past understandings to reach his full potential. A Family Reading is a tool to aid the individuals within the family to reach their full potential.

The question of the manner of death (withdrawal) was also discussed. The readings refer to death as withdrawal, meaning the attention is withdrawn from the conscious mind back into the subconscious mind. The subconscious mind is where you reside between lifetimes.

Questions were asked concerning creative abilities of the members of the family in the past lifetime. These individuals may have dormant understandings of art, music, and creativity that are just waiting to be expressed given the right stimulus. When asked if any special gifts or talents other than those mentioned in the early part of a reading could be elaborated upon, the response was full-bodied:

> *"We see there are many. We see upon the part of the one presently referred to as Tonya for there to be keen insights that this one has. We see for this one to be clairvoyant. We see for there to be many instances where this one can perceive probabilities of future events. We see that this one is excellent with organization and this one can work with people and cause there to be the meeting of compatible needs.*
>
> *We see upon the part of the one presently referred to as Debora for there to be a high degree of sensitivity that this one has developed to the needs of others and we see for this one to have the skill of listening. We see that this is well developed when this one wants to use it. This one does not always choose to do so.*
>
> *We see upon the part of Avram that there is once again the ability to be very focused, to be concentrated. We see capabilities for discrimination in terms of being able to identify what will work and what will not work.*
>
> *We see upon the part of the one presently referred to as Anna, that there is the nurturing capabilities that have already been described and the ability to embrace whatever this one puts the attention upon, whether this is a person, or a skill, something physical.*
>
> *We see upon the part of the one presently referred to as Charles that there is the capability of great problem solving, of reasoning. We see that this one can be very strong in terms*

of holding the attention upon one thing for an extended period of time. This one can be very determined.

We see that all of these ones have a kind of artistic flair in that they do express themselves creatively. There are ways which each one of them do utilize things in creative ways. They are different and they are not necessarily noticed by themselves but there has been some communication between them concerning this." (5-25-91-3-BGO)

With this family individual talents as well as those in common were described. Of the many different types of questions that can be asked during a reading, those which are deeply considered, honestly drawn, and sincerely asked will bring the greatest insight and joy when answered.

During Family Readings, questions are asked in order to aid the family in understanding their relationship to each other. Often the results are surprising, even shocking. Some Family Readings, by relating the individual causal factor of the attitudes of family members, explain the reason why members of a family have similar diseases. Thoughts are things and all cause, including dis-ease, begins with a thought. As children are being raised by their parents, they will usually be taught the habits and unproductive thinking of their parents as well as the productive experiences. These unproductive thought patterns over time can create disorder within the physical body. Thus, diseases that are said to be inherited are often inherited more mentally than physically. Sometimes the attitudes passed down from one generation to another leads to similar disease from a parent to son or from a daughter to grandchild. This family asked a question as to why most of these entities suffer from sinus difficulties.

"There is such secrecy of those things which they love and those things which they hold sacred for fear that if they express them they will lose them. This is the attitude and the restriction within their own spirit that causes the physical difficulty in sinuses as well as some constriction within the breathing and the air passages within the lungs....By using what was suggested in this information about expressing themselves and their dreams and those things which they

love and hold sacred this can change. (By) expressing these,
they will find that they will not lose them but that these things
will begin to become real in their lives and it will also release
the restriction within the bodies that they express as this
difficulty that they speak of." (2-9-87-1-CSR)

The exciting and fascinating answer given here opens a new area of
understanding of family held diseases. Previously it was thought that
these diseases were physically hereditary. We now find that some, if not
many of them, are created from attitudes passed down from parents to
children through generations. By breaking the chain of unproductive
attitudes and by teaching individual family members to be more
productive in their thinking and attitudes, the chain of cause is changed.

A reading for a mother and her two adult daughters included a
question concerning the physical health of one of the daughters, Karen.
Karen, who was adopted, has cerebral palsy.   The mother asked for
suggestions that might help all three of them to better cope with this
disorder. The response is enlightening as it reveals the karmic nature of
the daughter's condition.

"Would suggest first, to the other two it would be important
for these ones to realize that they have not caused this
disorder and therefore in that way are not responsible for it.
If this is understood, then there can be a freedom in the
choices made according to what these two want to give to the
one of the other. It would be important for these ones to
remember that whatever they do choose to offer is something
that is given because they so desire and this would be the idea
to keep uppermost in mind.

Upon the part of the one presently referred to as Karen, we
see that this is at a stage where this one could adjust the
attitudes to such a way as to cause there to be a difference in
the ways that it manifests and even a change in the quality
and caliber of the physical strength. We see that this one is
very strong-willed and therefore this is a great asset in this
one being able to cause there to be a change in this disorder.
We see that the will, however, has been allowed to be
stubborn rather than directed by intelligence and thereby
will-power. This one has many available opportunities to

express the intelligence she holds and we see that with the
discipline and directed use of the intelligence there could be
great changes effected. This would need to be a desire upon
this one's part, however, for as in the past lifetime related,
this one has fought discipline throughout the life, and there
would need to be a change in this. It is because of the fighting
in part that this one has manifested this disorder in the life.
It is therefore a challenge for this one to meet, and the
challenge is no greater than this one is." (5-23-91-18-BGO)

One Family Reading was given for a family composed of a husband, wife, and three daughters. At the time of the reading all five were adults. The husband-father in the present time period was about to die, or what is referred to in readings as "withdraw from the physical". In talking with one of the daughters, I learned she was very happy to have received this reading before her father died. She used the information to understand and come to terms with many aspects of her family and her growing up years that would not have been possible otherwise.

The woman knew that we do not do readings on someone who has withdrawn from the physical. Our duty is to aid the people in the physical to become whole, functioning Selves. The physical is the place you build permanent understandings that you carry with you from lifetime to lifetime. Because the reading was timely for the conditions in this family, the daughter continues to have this information about her past to aid her in being more productive in the present long after her father's death.

Although a family member who is no longer alive cannot be included in the Family Reading, significant information has been gained concerning the living family member's attitudes about a death in the family. A reading for a mother and her children did not include her recently deceased husband, but a question asked provided significant insight into the husband/father's relationship with the family both from the past lifetime and the present. It offered insight to the children concerning their father's death:

"We see in the past lifetime related this one that has been
queried (the husband/father) was the mother in concern that
has been described. The experience of the ones presently

*referred to as Angelique and Catharina was very similar to
the one in the past lifetime related where there was the kind
of distance for the reasons that have already been stated.
We see that in the present time period there is a similar kind
of attitude that these ones have. In part it is a kind of distance
that they experience now, a kind of definiteness of finality, a
kind of yearning for something that cannot occur, a kind of
desire for communication which they feel has been thwarted
– at least this is true for the one of Angelique – or a kind of
apathy or giving up in what they do desire to change. (There
is the impression that what) they would have desired cannot
now occur. Would suggest that upon each one of these one's
parts that this is not so, that these ideas that have been
described are stimuli for these ones to think more completely,
to cause there to be understanding brought into their existence
so that they themselves can be different and the relationships
that they have in their life can be different. Would suggest
that it be looked at in this way.*

*Would suggest also that the reality of their existence is not
quite as final as these ones would see it and there is still the
available opportunity for communication, that there is still
the openness for learning and for exchange of love. Would
suggest that these ones recognize that whatever is given in
this way with intention does fulfill a purpose and it is a reality
that these ones can experience." (5-23-91-18-BGO)*

Through the many years of providing readings, I have repeatedly discovered and been reminded of their unlimited value, not only for the people immediately receiving the reading but for anyone who is invested in the progression of their soul. The insights from this reading concerning the understanding of life and death are universally applicable and can be useful to anyone. When studied as a body of research material, Family Readings also reveal the universal threads which form the bonds of giving and receiving between independent souls.

Each individual and every family has the right and duty to understand who they are, where they came from, where they are going, why they have chosen to incarn with a specific family, and where and when they have been with this family before. Family Readings may present past life associations in such varied places and time periods as

France in the 1700's, England in the 1600's, China in the 1100's, Egypt 500 B.C., India 700 B.C., Peru in 500 A.D, or Atlantis in 10,000 B.C. Each past life association from a Family Reading will have its own time period and location. You can explore real history, not one the historians have recorded from their point of view, rather one relative to you and your family's past life history.

Daniel R. Condron, D.M., D.D., M.S., was born in Chillicothe, Missouri. Raised on a farm ten miles from that town, he excelled in sports and academics during his high school years. Condron furthered his education at the University of Missouri-Columbia where he earned Bachelors and Masters degrees. He traveled through Europe and South America, and was named to Who's Who in American Colleges and Universities.

Dr. Condron has devoted the last thirty years of his life to Self awareness and to understanding the Universal Language of Mind. He considers the spreading of this language his assignment for this lifetime. In order for there to be world peace, there must not only be peace in each individual, there must also be a universal language to communicate the peace and understanding of one individual to another. Toward this end he is writing a series of books on **The Universal Language of Mind** *as applied to the symbolic books in the Bible. He has written several other books including* **Dreams of the Soul** *on the Yogi Sutras of Patanjali and* **Permanent Healing** *which was the subject of his major address during the 1993 Parliament of the World's Religions.*

As a teacher of mind and spirit, Dr. Condron has shared his knowledge with thousands through formal study, seminars, and conferences, and literally millions through media around the globe. He is chancellor of the College of Metaphysics and serves as President of the Board of Directors of the School of Metaphysics. He is listed in Who's Who in the Midwest and Who's Who of Professionals. His influence continues to reach around the world as a conductor of readings. Dr. Condron looks forward to aiding millions more people to lead a richer and more rewarding life.

Family Reading Transcripts

F amily Readings are phenomenal. The insights they reveal about how family members influence and affect one another are astounding.

In about an hour, a Family Reading will paint a complete picture of the family members including their past and present association. The past life association is described revealing the members' relativity to one another. Repeated patterns of thought and behavior, both productive and destructive to selves and the family, are identified. The reading describes the causes of loyalties, affections, openness, jealousies, resentments, rivalries. Whatever dynamics exist in the family, there is a reason for their presence which revolves around the needs of the souls of those involved. Family Readings go straight to the heart of the group's karmic obligations, and in this way answer many questions for those involved.

Family Readings are similar to Past Life Crossing of Paths which are between two people. However, Family Readings are much more involved because they must trace the paths of up to five people, seeking a place where all five were previously in association. Since souls tend to incarnate with the same souls over time, in most cases, a lifetime can be found where the present family members did indeed know one another. Sometimes they were family members in the past, sometimes they were business or schooling associates, and sometimes they are a mixture of the two. As is true with all past life readings, what the past relationships are is fascinating. How they are significant to the present family is often compelling.

Two individuals have given us permission to publish the entire transcript of their Family Readings in hopes that they will aid even one reader to a deeper understanding of his or her own familial relations. These readings demonstrate the different combinations of related people who can receive this type of reading. To make it easier for you to follow these elements, the people in each reading are described according to their relationship with the person requesting the reading. They also demonstrate the elements created when more than two people are involved. The first reading is for a complete family unit: a son requesting a reading with his father, mother, and older sister. Very different from this, the second reading is for five women: two sisters and their three daughters.

First, the Family Reading for Jason will be presented in its entirety enabling you to experience a reading as it is related. Comments by the person who requested this reading will follow. The second reading will be presented in a different manner that we will describe later. Now, for the Family Reading of Jason, a twenty-six year old computer specialist from the Midwest. The younger of two children, Jason was born and raised in Omaha, Nebraska. When he was 14, his parents divorced and he lived with his father in the childhood home. At 18, he left home to go to college and has been on his own since. Jason requested this reading two years ago, in the hopes of gaining further understanding of himself and his family members.

You will search for a significant crossing of paths with this one referred to as Jason and those referred to as Father and Mother and Sister and relate that significant crossing for these four entities.

We see for these ones to be within the area referred to as China. We see for these ones to have come together when a marriage was arranged between the one referred to presently as Jason and the one presently referred to as Father. We see that the one referred to presently as Father was in female form at that time. We see for the female to have entered into the household of the husband, the one presently referred to as Jason, and we see for there to have been conflict immediately between the one presently referred to as Father and the one presently referred to as Sister. We see for the one presently referred to as Sister to have been the sister of the one presently referred to as Jason. We see for the two women to have clashed and we see for them to have experienced jealousies and envies in their physical situation.

We see that the one presently referred to as Sister did not believe that she would marry. We see that there had been several attempts to arrange this but there had been something that would occur, whether it would be the death of the intended spouse, or some other offer that would be made to the intended spouse that would be better or would be taken, and this left her without a mate. We see that this had occurred several times and that she had begun to believe that she would never marry. We see therefore that she did not want her siblings to marry either, particularly this particular brother because this one was very attached to him and was very fond of him, and did want to control his life.

We see that in many ways she did view the one presently referred to as Jason as a substitute for the husband she did not have. We see that there was not any overt physical affection between them or sexual involvement but we see that in her mind she did rely upon the one presently referred to as Jason for protection, and for many of the securities that she would have expected from the one of a husband. We see therefore when the wife was brought into the household that she very much resented this and we see that she did try to undermine the marriage.

We see that the one presently referred to as Father, the wife, was very meek and was introverted, therefore it took her a while to realize the amount of animosity that was being directed toward her. We see that she was not very versed in being able to defend herself and was fairly ignorant of her even being attacked for she had been sheltered in her young life. We see that when she became aware of this she did not know how to interpret it, and therefore did not understand it for a number of years. We see the one presently referred to as Jason was ignorant of all of this occurring, and we see that he continued to merely do what he wanted to do in regards to his sister and in regards to his wife. We see when the wife did eventually understand that the sister held such jealousy toward her we see that she tried to tell her husband about this, but her husband being inattentive to the interplay between the two women merely passed it off as it being of her imagination.

We see that when she learned that she would not gain any assistance or protection from her husband, the one of the wife did begin to imagine ways to retaliate to the sister, and we see one of these to be giving her husband something that the sister could not, and that was a child. We see that the child was born and it was presently referred to as Mother. We see that the child was female. And we see that this again added another element to the dynamics of the relationship between all of these ones for it was another female force which as she grew older learned the *jealousies and the introversion of the two primary females in her life. And we see that in effect it was the female child that began to gain all the attention of the male.*

As the years progressed, this caused the sister and the wife to lower their resistance to one another, and begin to work in cooperation with one another. We see they did view the relationship between the father and daughter as unhealthy. We see that they were actually jealous of the closeness between the two. And that their jealousies undermined the closeness by beginning to undermine the reputation of the male. We see this was intentional upon their part and it was in an attempt to compensate for their hurt.

We see that there were thoughts within the sister's and wife's mind of being owed something from the one of the male. They both felt they were not given what they should have been given and in their actions they would force this kind of attention from the one of the male. We see that this actually caused greater discord and disharmony, and eventually when the male became somewhat more aware of what was occurring he felt betrayed by both his sister and his wife. This caused more distance between himself and these females, rather than the closeness that these females had intended.

We see that since the daughter was reaching adult years when this was transpiring she did side with her father and we see that she was more acutely aware of the intentions of the sister and her mother. We see she did try to explain these to the male but the male had decided that it was beyond his comprehension of why the females would think or behave in such a manner and he would not listen to her. Therefore he remained ignorant throughout the incarnation. We see that in effect he would wash his hands of anything that he felt was unpleasant or he did not understand, and we see that in doing so this one merely fed the difficulty rather than being a tool for the resolve. We see eventually, as the daughter grew into adult years, she began to hold some disrespect for her father because of these attitudes. And we see she began talking more and more with her mother and with her aunt. We see that the three women did communicate and did gain some understanding of their situation.

We see that a marriage was arranged for the daughter. We see initially she was against this but she did end up embracing it. It did remove her from this household. We see that this did ease some of the tensions for a period of time but we see by that time the females had become resistant to any kind of advance that the male would make.

We see that they were acutely aware that his advances were tenders of communications or affection or merely because of his own loneliness because the daughter was no longer in the household. And we see they were not very open or receptive to this. We see the one of the male once again did not understand this and did not make really any attempts to do so. We see for the one of the male to have withdrawn first within these relationships. We see for this to have been from respiratory difficulties. We see for this to have been at the age of 41. We see for him to have been referred to as Wang Gai Nong.

We see for the one presently referred to as Sister, the one of his sister during this time period, to have withdrawn next. We see for this to have been at the age of 47. We see for that one to have been referred to as Chi Ka.

We see for the one presently referred to as Father, the wife during this time period, to have withdrawn at the age of 50. We see for that one to have been referred to as Ta Lien.

We see for the one of the other, the one presently referred to as Mother, the daughter during this time period, to have withdrawn at the age of 34. We see that this was in childbirth. And we see for her to have been referred to as La Fong.

We see for this time period to be 430 B.C. This is all.

Were there any more children born between these two during that time period?

We see that there were a total of seven children born but only four did reach adult years.

Were these both male and female?

Yes.

And what was the one of the father in that time period, what were his thoughts and attitudes towards the ones of the sons?

We see that initially the sons were seen as a refuge by this one. We see that because he had such difficulties with the females in his life he did seek to gravitate toward the male sons. And we see that initially this was comforting to him, but as the sons grew older and became somewhat opinionated, judgmental, and rebellious in terms of himself he did not know how to respond to this and began to see the sons in the same light that he saw the females in his life and removed himself from them and did not deal with them and did not think about them in great depth or with intention.

What was the manner of withdrawal for each of these four entities related in this time period?

This has been given for two of them. We see for the one presently referred to as Sister for this to have been food poisoning. We see for the one presently referred to as Father for this to have been kidney failure.

Very well, what would be the significance of that lifetime to the present lifetime for these four entities?

We see once again for the commonality between these ones to be in how they are motivated. We see that once again there is a need for external motivation for all of them to be able to move forward in their thinking. We see that they are often prone to falling into rash decisions or opinions which actually do not have much of a foundation, and we see that in doing so these ones rely upon each other for support of their opinions or beliefs.

We see that many times as was in the past this is not in a productive sense to find courage in confidence in being able to produce, rather it is in being able to justify their limitations. We see that this is true for each one of these ones and we see them to reach out in a least line of resistance to the other within the group that will side with them in effect, that will support their limitations and their justifications and in that way create fostering of this kind of weakness.

We see that there is a great sense of connection that these ones have.

There is a very real sense of bonding that these ones have. And we see that no matter what disagreements they may entertain or what kinds of conflicts arise, it does not hinder the bond. We see however that there is an attempt upon these one's part once again to expect a kind of magical revelation from the bond in producing understanding. As was in the past this did not occur, and it does not occur in the present. We see that there is some need on each one of these one's parts to recognize that understanding is the result of individual desire and effort. It is not something that occurs merely because situations force the self into understanding. We see that each one of these ones are capable of much greater understanding than they give themselves credit for in the present time period and we see that each would benefit from the growth that would occur in pursuing understanding. We see that there is some tendency upon their thinking to believe that something will be lost if understanding is pursued. And indeed there will be changes in the way they see themselves and the way they see the life. However this is not a loss but a transformation of awareness and it needs to be seen as such.

We see that specifically, once again, upon the part of the one presently referred to as Jason, that there is the tendency to become removed and distant in regards to the interactions with the others. There is the tendency when a conflict arises or something that this one does not understand occurs for this one to turn the back upon these situations rather than to face them courageously and gain understanding. This one needs to learn how to extend the self in relationships rather than to back away or to run from what is unpleasant. We see that this will aid this one in being able to create a fuller realization of responsibility for self and for the life.

We see that in regards to the one presently referred to as Father that there is once again the tendency to allow the self to be buffeted by situations and relationships around him. And we see that this one holds a somewhat stubborn stance in regards to this one's sense of who he is or his identity, but this one is highly influenced by the other people in this one's life, more so than they are aware of. And we see that this is because in spite of this one's show of being very stubborn or very opinionated this one is in reality very indecisive and waits for conditions around the self to form this one's ideas, as this one did in the past. And we see that this causes this one to accomplish much less than what this one is capable of and it creates much frustration not only within this group but within the life as well for this one does not really know the purpose of his existence and is not finding the life satisfying or fulfilling because of this. In order for this to occur this one would need to become much more contemplative and reflective in terms of this one's ideals, and in terms of what this one really thinks about that which this one values. This one does need to learn to initiate communication.

We see upon the part of the one presently referred to as Sister that this one is very dynamic and is very aggressive in this one's thoughts and interrelationships. And we see that this one needs to recognize the very powerful influence that this one has upon others. We see that this one discounts this and merely becomes short-sighted and narrow in vision in this one wanting to have what she wants. And this one then uses the influence to accomplish it, but she has very little awareness of how this is affecting her life in a grander scale and how this affects the lives of others. This group could enhance this one's ability to understand this, and to recognize that this one's influence today will continue to remain in the future that it is not just momentary but that it does exist over a prolonged period of time.

We see for the one presently referred to as Mother that there is once again attachment. It is an attachment to all of these individuals and we see that it is not always held equally in one time period. We see that this one changes the loyalties very easily and we see that this causes this one some dissatisfaction within the self. We see that this one feels a need to be protected and feels a need to be taken care of. And this one will gravitate toward whichever individual in this group is offering this to her. We see that this is a way in which this one fosters the weakness and lack of confidence within the self. And as this one would be willing to initiate some change in this one's perspective this one would be able to understand more what this one has to offer in this group. This one loses sight of what she has of value to offer these other ones. And when this occurs this one will either become sullen and introspective or scattered in this one's feverish attempts to gain value, or will become pompous and controlling in this one's attempt to prove the value.

We see that it would be of benefit for all of these ones to begin to contemplate and integrate into their thinking the recognition that the organization of the thoughts that they hold are individual, that there is not another to blame for the thoughts that they hold. And that there is not another to give credit to for the thoughts that they hold. In this way these ones need to learn individual responsibility for their thoughts and what their thoughts create. We see that when conflict arises within this group whether it is between two or more of them it tends to gravitate and center upon this lack of understanding. We see that they tend to fall into blaming one another for conditions and circumstances. They fail to see how they are merely seeing a mirrored reflection of their own attitudes. And therefore there is stagnation that is achieved in their relating with one another, and in their own growth.

Would suggest that these ones take the perspective of recognizing that much of the difficulty is due to a projection of their own thinking upon someone else, and that as these ones learn to admit their own thinking there will be a greater opportunity for them to separate their thoughts from that of the others. Only when this occurs will they truly be able to discover each other as individuals. Until then they will rely upon past experience, memories, prejudices, and biases in regard to one another and will not actually know who the others are or who they are.

We see that in combination for the most, each of these ones can be imaginative, each one of these ones can dream, each one of these ones can hold ideals and can envision situations and circumstances beyond what they experience. Each one also shares a weakness in will power in being able to make these ideals and dreams come about. And this is much of the source of irritation that they find with one another.

We see that once again there is a tendency towards jealousy upon the parts of the ones of Sister and Father, and to a lesser degree upon the part of Mother. And this does tend to create a restriction in any of these ones fulfilling their ideals. For when there is movement towards this, when there is the use of creation, when there is the manifestation of dreams, desires, and ideals upon any one of these one's parts there is a tendency for one or more of the others to side against that one or to become jealous or to try to tear down what that one is doing. This is a highly negative and destructive element that does exist within this group, because it exists within each one of them, even the one presently referred to as Jason. In fact, probably more so in that one because that one becomes so ignorant of his own motivations and his own relationships with the others. This is a kind of illness and disease that exists within them as individuals and comes to bear within their interactions with one another that could very easily be healed as these ones would begin to pursue the kind of individual and inner development that has been suggested throughout the significance given. This is all.

The one of Mother, that is the third vibration, says "Is there any remaining karma I need to resolve in my relationship with any member of my family? If there is, what is the best way I may complete that learning?"

Information has been given in that regard, not only in regards to this one directly and personally, but also in regards to the commonalties in attitudes that this one shares with the others. There are no further suggestions.

She also says "What skills, talents, and abilities could I best draw from my past lives that would help me right now in my life?"

Would suggest that these are apparent to this one in what comes naturally to her. We see that as this one would begin to admit those qualities, abilities, and skills which this one possesses rather than to hide them or put them down as is this one's tendency in the insecurities that have already been described in detail for this one, then there would be a greater recognition of her own value and a greater recognition of the benefit of experience whether in this lifetime or in previous lifetimes.

This one also says "What is my soul's purpose for this lifetime?"

We see that there is a need to understand loyalty. There is a need to understand the ability to become committed to a particular line of thinking. There is a need to distinguish between pretense and existence.

This one says "How may I give of myself to aid in my family's growth?"

In the ways that have already been described.

This one says "What were the causes or reasons that broke my marriage with Father, and are there any lessons to be learned from that experience?"

We see that because of the stagnation which has already been spoken of that does exists within this entire group that there were choices made which resulted in a change in the dynamics of the association in regards to the one of Mother. We see that this one was not able to receive from the one of Father what she desired, and we see that after attempting to take from him those things desired over a period of time that this was eventually released. We see that this one however has not found a way to give to the self what this one feels was lacking, and there is still an attachment to someone else giving what this one feels she needs to her, rather than this one being able to give it to herself.

The one of Jason, that is the first vibration says "What is my soul's purpose for this lifetime?"

We see that in part in as much as it related to this group that this one needs to learn the essence of duty and the spirit of responsibility.

This one also says "Why do I react to my father when we communicate?"

This one very easily falls into not understanding, just as this one did in the past lifetime related, and we see that there is irritation there. We see that this one expects the other one to be a certain way, and when he is not then this one shuts down communication.

Which one shuts down, the one of Jason or the one of the other?

The one of Jason. We see that this is also what the one presently referred to as Father does, but we see that the question was in regards to the one of Jason.

This one of Jason also says "What are some qualities that I may draw from within myself that I could use to build my relationship with my sister?"

It would aid this one a great deal to build substance. This would be in regards to this one's ideas. This one needs to experience the ideas purposefully so that when this one interacts with others, then there can be a kind of confidence and a kind of quiet surety within the self. This is lacking for the most part, and interactions with the one of the other tend to accentuate this.

He also says "What role has my mother played in my spiritual development this lifetime?"

We see that in many ways these ones have very similar issues. They do tend to gravitate toward one another and even side with each other against the others within this group. We see that in as much as they are very much alike in that regard, and that they both have similar issues of insecurity, lack of confidence, and the need to understand loyalty, there is much potential for stimulation and growth. (10-6-92-1-BGC)

"When I first heard of Family Readings I became very interested in having one done on my family. I was excited to know where my family was together in the past, and what our association was. My parents were divorced over 10 years ago, and there has been a great need by all for greater understanding and harmony. I began to share my desire and bring a consensus among my family members that this Family Reading was a great thing to do.

"My dad was a mechanical engineer for AT&T and mom was a housewife. My sister was 17 off in college when they divorced. I stayed with my father. At first it was okay, but we didn't get along too well. There was a lot of fighting between us, and I wasn't there a whole lot. There were periods of time when we were communicating more and there were periods of time when we wouldn't. He had a terrible temper and would get angry quite often about trivial things. I consequently had a distaste for even being around him after a while." In the past lifetime Jason's association with his father was through an arranged marriage, in the present lifetime as he describes it, the relationship was arranged due to the divorce.

"In many ways I could communicate more openly with my mother at that time. It was about a three year period where this went on and I visited my mother about twice a week and that was a pretty regular schedule." This is reflective of Jason's turning from his wife and sister in that past life and siding with his daughter.

Listening to him speak, it seemed curious to me that Jason would not have stayed with his mother following the divorce in the present lifetime. He said, "I thought about moving in with my mother, however, I guess it was more physical thinking. That house was where my home was and that's where I wanted to be. You know, there was more stuff there. I could have friends over. It gave me different opportunities to socialize with people than it would have if I would have been in the apartment with my mother. I wouldn't have had the same kind of resources." Once again Jason was ignoring the people in his family, their desires and fears, wants and jealousies.

"In the reading, I was the father and I was apparently just a tyrant in that lifetime. I eventually estranged all of my family except for my sister who is also my sister in this lifetime. And I've maintained an excellent association with her, with the exception of recently when my father had a stroke but we are back on good terms again." That breach was actually foreshadowed by the reading: *"We see that there were thoughts within the sister's* [present-day sister] *and wife's* [present-day father] *mind of being owed something from the one of the male. They both felt they were not given what they should have been given and in their actions they would force this kind of attention from the one of the male."*

Even with the sister's jealousies of the other women in her brother's life, she still stayed with him throughout the previous life. That long-standing friendship between brother and sister in the past continues into the present, "There has always been a mutual liking and attraction as a friend. We talk to each other as in that past lifetime. She stuck with me all the way to the end. She was someone who I associated with and maintained good relations with."

There are also parallels in the life of the present-day mother who in the past life was Jason's daughter. In the present, Jason's mother left the family when she divorced his father. In the past life, "After she had a chance to move away from the area, she married, there was not a lot of association with the family."

As in the past life, Jason was often oblivious to the interactions of family members and their emotional impact. *"We see the one presently referred to as Jason was ignorant of all of this occurring, and we see that he continued to merely do what he wanted to do in regards to his sister and in regards to his wife"* …. *"her husband being inattentive to the interplay between the two women merely passed it off as it being of her imagination"* ….and…… *"the male had decided that it was beyond his comprehension of why the females would think or behave in such a manner and he would not listen to her. Therefore he remained ignorant throughout the incarnation."*

In the present lifetime, Jason has this to say about his father, "He doesn't communicate his thoughts openly. It's all just emotion. And that's why you are left wondering, 'What the hell are you thinking?' He would never answer that question. He would change the subject. He would always make us laugh. I had a very happy upbringing up until my early teen years.

There seemed to be a lot of harmony between my mother and father. I never really saw them fight. It was only in those later years when that started to happen."

"Looking back on it, my father tended to rebel against authority. He would always put down his boss. He hated cops. He didn't like authority and I grew up with an image of this and so my respect for authority was not – there was a need for learning there and a need for understanding structure too." The reading describes this "*in spite of this one's show of being very stubborn or very opinionated this one is in reality very indecisive and waits for conditions around the self to form this one's ideas....And we see that this causes this one to accomplish much less than what this one is capable of and it creates much frustration not only within this group but within the life as well for this one does not really know the purpose of his existence and is not finding the life satisfying or fulfilling because of this.*" Jason comments, "I don't think he understood or liked certain parts of his life, like his work life particularly. I think he felt restricted and thus conveyed that attitude to me. I know he wanted to open a knife sharpening business and I know he never fulfilled that desire.

"I've always been interested in starting my own business. Even at a young age I started to take activity on that and he never supported me. He always would find something wrong with what I did and ultimately I overcame that because I didn't let that discourage me. I continued to make choices to do what I felt I wanted to do." Jason's description of these father-son dynamics are reminiscent of the reading's assessment of himself: "*We see that this one* [Jason] *expects the other one* [father] *to be a certain way, and when he is not then this one shuts down communication.*"

Even so, Jason says the reading helped him to accept his father as a person rather than just his dad. "It was a shock that I was married to my father in a past life. It really totally changed my perspective of life. It did help me to gain objectivity. And it definitely helped me see him as a person or as an adult, a man who made choices. The reading helped me to understand that the restrictions that he had were with him. They were not me. It helped me to separate and identify who I am and these other issues that are his issues that are not me. The reading [helped me to] look at him as a man who has made choices in his life who ended up at point B and point A because of his choices."

It is interesting to note that in the past lifetime Jason estranged his daughter, and in the present lifetime Jason felt his father estranged him.

This is clearly an indication of Jason's karmic obligation; he has the opportunity to experience what he previously caused another to suffer. Concerning his present life, Jason says the estrangement from his father "stimulated my desire to want to get to know him more. He had a stroke about a year and a half ago. I've moved within easy driving distance of him and I spend anywhere from one to four times a month visiting him. Going out to dinner, associating with him, asking questions, being with him emotionally. Being there, being with him."

Jason quickly admits before the health problems he saw his father "as little as possible. There really was no desire to even reach out because there was no communication. But now I see it as a soul, as a learning opportunity, not whether this is pleasant or unpleasant. So maybe it's uncomfortable sometimes, so what. He's my father. This is what I'm here to learn about. And I have a duty that transcends my pleasure or not pleasure with the association. It has become a lot more pleasant because there are things that he does have that I want to learn. And I've not always admitted that. His understandings of his relationships with people are not very great. He does have great ethics in responsibility for his family and his life. Even though he divorced his wife he was very responsible for us kids and he cared for us a great deal in the best way he knew how, which was financially. He did that very well.

"The reading helped to stimulate me to reflect on the fact that I am a soul, not a physical body. It helped me to gain objectivity into what it is I wanted to do with my father. You know, not just being with him, but there is a purpose. I'm learning about how to open up and how to ask questions, and how to communicate and how to reach out to someone and care, and risk that. And I was never taught that by him so I am going into territory that is foreign to both of us, foreign to the family. The reading helped me realize we need more understanding, there needs to be more communication. There is this big block. A lot of pretense. I think my father and mother fell in love with each other the way that they wanted them to be, not the way they actually were. In the past lifetime theirs was a mother-daughter relationship and they held an image of the way the person ought to be. It was a similar dynamic that obviously is repeating itself."

Another pattern emerges concerning Jason's sister and his present day father [his past lifetime wife]. In the past the two women bonded together against Jason. A bonding between the two has once again occurred since Jason's father suffered a stroke and subsequently moved into his daughter's household for care. "That bonding is exactly true. That's the same pattern. They have definitely bonded together. And in a way I was kind of the enemy for a while. Not any more. What I've done different this lifetime is I have initiated communication with both of them and that household. I am initiating, reaching out, communicating, inviting them to do things, asking questions. I didn't do that in the past life. I just didn't mess with them at all. But now I'm using my will and imagination to change that and I'm initiating a new association with them."

Dynamics repeat themselves for Jason's mother as well. In the past life, she was Jason's daughter who grew up, married, and left the family. From that time on she was not really related to what was going on in the household. This is relevant to what has occurred in the present since she divorced her husband and moved out of the homestead. "I incarned in a family where my father and mother simply didn't communicate and they were both too stubborn to admit anything. It took me a long time to realize that this is their choice as people. And it's okay to accept them for that. I don't think I did that in the last lifetime I accepted them for who they were. I just kept my fixed image and it just went on. That's something I'm doing different in this lifetime. I'm not maintaining that fixed image of who they used to be. I'm respecting who they are but I'm still associating with them. I'm not disassociating. I'm making efforts.

"With my mother, I initiate a call to her quite often. Because I feel like she has this thought form that she's outside the family but she puts herself there. Even though I consistently call her and talk to her, she's so touched that I call her. And it's like 'Jeez, I'm not fifty million miles away.' I can tell that there's that distance there. I think she feels victimized still in some ways. In some ways she has told me that she understands that she had to leave because she felt it was emotionally abusive to be in the [marriage] relationship, but her contact with her children afterwards, it's like she is timid. She is not confident in herself to initiate contact. Once in a while she might invite us to something but it's like she is just timid. I have initiated more communication with her. I think in the past lifetime there was a lack of that. I think as my daughter in that lifetime I did not initiate communication.

"In regards to my sister, even though she is married in the present lifetime, the aspect of the jealousy arises again. In a way I was kind of jealous of the bond and the association that my sister and my father were forming [during his recovery]. But instead of remaining jealous what I'm choosing to do now is to reach out and that's having a whole different effect.

They are trusting me more now. I'm spending time with my father alone. Which is definitely a trust on their part because my sister and her husband are very protective of him. I'm also learning about being more caring and considering others and being less self centered."

Most of this reading centers around Jason and his relationships with the other three. This often occurs in a Family Reading; the person requesting the reading is the one most invested in receiving and using the information and so s/he is most open to what is given. As has been described, Jason has become more aware of his family's thoughts and feelings, more sensitive to their needs and desires both individually and somewhat collectively. There is a sense of a newfound maturity in how Jason looks at his family's past, their present, and their future. "I think in America in a lot of dysfunctional families, as the popular psychologists call it, these Family Readings are essential in overcoming any blocks in communication that a family may be experiencing and to get specific suggestions to change those. In our reading the core suggestion was to ask questions of each other to pursue greater understanding which really I've done quite consciously. I am leading the way in my family in doing that, I don't believe the others have followed suit. Yet."

When Jason describes his family's responses to their reading it is quite clear why he is the one who received the most insight from the reading and therefore has benefited the most. "My sister read it and she really didn't trust in the validity of it and didn't want to give it much credit. She was upset that she had to use her married name because she has chosen to keep her maiden name. [From years of experience in gaining this information from the inner levels, the most recent husband's last name is used during the reading for a woman who has been married in order to gain the most accurate information possible.] So that established her bias right from the start.

"My mother, surprisingly, was not sure whether or not and how much to accept. I know she believes in the Edgar Cayce readings implicitly and even though what we are doing is extremely similar...I think that it is just ego because she also got a Health Analysis which was obviously accurate. If she would have found it on her own maybe her attitude would have been different. But since it's coming from her son, I think she still has an image of her as a teacher to me. In many ways she was a spiritual teacher for me. I mean she taught me a lot of things about metaphysics at a pretty young age that opened me up to those ideas. And now I'm offering her things that she wasn't aware of."

Self disclosure is the heart of the readings offered through the School of Metaphysics.   When someone is not inclined toward self revelation and inner change, it is easy to reject the insights presented by questioning the source. About his mother Jason said, "She has never been comfortable with self disclosure. She will if I'm just listening to her. She'll kind of let a little bit out. I used to try to give her advice when she did that and that merely angered her. She didn't like that so now I'm just listening. Just listening and not trying to push anything at her. My dad never heard or read the reading at all."

For those considering a Family Reading Jason emphasizes that "the major issues of learning that you're in the family to gain will be brought out into the open. In our case it was the need for understanding. In a lot of families there is not that open communication of what they are feeling or what their thoughts are. Not emotional dumping but what their thoughts are. What are you thinking? Open up. There are a lot of difficulties with communication that can be understood and changed for the better.

"It will help to approach the reading from a point of exploration and curiosity, make sure all the attitudes are in the right places. And when you are listening to the reading don't say well, 'I knew you were that way.' Don't do any of that. Just be loving to each other when you are listening to the reading and that will encourage everybody to open up and trust each other and there will be a lot more growth from it."

The "Gentle" Women

The following Family Reading was conducted for the women in a family, two sisters and their three daughters. The moniker "Gentle" women has a dual meaning for these women, one relevant to blood relation and the other description of the consciousness of the quintessential woman from the Southern United States which intriguingly comes through even in the context of Babylonia 23 centuries before the birth of Jesus.

For the purposes of this book, those included in the reading are referred to by their first name and their relationship to Sue, the woman submitting the request. Therefore, we have Sue, Sue's mother and sister, and Sue's aunt and cousin. As you will see the significant lifetime related for these women is both exciting in content and rich in understanding.

Rather than wait til the entire reading is given, Sue's commentary is placed as relevant information is given.

The reason why Sue pursued the reading is a story unto itself. "I got that reading because I was having a lot of problems in relation to my cousin, RJ. My cousin was like the princess, not unlike her role in the past lifetime as it turned out. She was like a model. She always had her fingernails done, her hair done. And everybody just kind of revolved around RJ, and how RJ felt, what RJ wanted. It was like an unspoken service to RJ. And the reason I had this reading done is that at one point I just realized that anytime RJ and I were in relation with each other it was what *I* could do for *her*. What I had that she needed, or how basically I could be of service to her. What I really desired was for RJ to care more about me, who I was, how I was doing. I wanted her to just care on a level of 'How are you, Sue? What's going on in your life? Can we share on that level, on a heart level?'

"It was coming down to 'Sue, we're going to be making June [RJ's mother] a garden. Can you and Bob [Sue's husband] bring your pickup truck and all your garden tools and come help us?' That was just kind of like the straw that broke the camel's back. It was like, 'No, you can go rent tools at Aztec for nothing.' When this was brought up and I said this to her, it was as if I just shot somebody. It was like, 'How dare you say no to me!' It really put a thorn in her side that I would not serve her. This was why I got the reading, to get a deeper understanding of the nature of our relationships so that I could have some kind of understanding to work with."

Sue said she wanted to get a Family Reading rather than just a Past Life Crossing with RJ "because these are the 'Gentle' women. There was always a bond that was between all of us. My mother and aunt's maiden name was Gentle. We were considered the Gentle clan and there is a whole attitude and process that goes on with the Gentle women. It's one of sticking together through thick and thin." And as you will see, this is exactly what these women did so many centuries ago.

You will search for a significant crossing of paths with this one referred to as Sue and that one referred to as Kathleen [sister], and that one referred to as Helen [aunt], and that one referred to as RJ [cousin] and that one referred to as Margorie [mother] and relate that significant crossing for these five entities.

We see these ones in female form. We see these ones to be within the area referred to as Babylonia. We see for them to have been in the same place, and we see for four of these ones to have been involved in the same activity. We see that the exception to this was the one presently referred to as RJ. We see that she was part of what could be termed the aristocracy. She was the daughter of one who held a position of power within this area. And we see therefore that she was one of the ones that were served by the other four. We see that she was considered somewhat simpleminded by her peers because she was kind of heart and generous. We see that she would communicate and associate with these other women. We see that the remainder of her peers saw this as degrading or as below them. But we see that this one, the one presently referred to as RJ, never did have this kind of attitude of being better than someone else; therefore she would often associate with those who were considered servants.

We see for the remaining four to be involved in the utilization of material. The material was used to clothe those that were in the aristocracy and we see that this was considered a duty as well as a position of service. It was part of their activities to mend, to perfume, to color, to prepare the clothing that the females within the aristocracy would adorn themselves with.

"In this lifetime, Aunt Helen and Cousin RJ both make quilts. They get old quilts and repair them. They also take blue jean fabrics and sew lace and buttons on it. They put ornaments on blue jeans, jackets, and skirts. I'm an aroma therapist, so what was then perfume I now work with in a different way. I've also done the sewing of lace on clothing and stuff like that. My sister Kathleen is a calligrapher and so is RJ. Kathleen learned it from RJ. Kathleen has also worked with RJ and has always learned from RJ as in that past life."

We see for the one presently referred to as Margorie to be the eldest of these four. She had been within this activity for a longer period of time than the others. Their ages were not widely disparate. We see that they were within ten years of the same age.

We see that the one presently referred to as Kathleen was the youngest and was the closest in age to that other one presently referred to as RJ.

These ones became almost friends over a period of time. And we see that the one presently referred to as Kathleen was fascinated by the one of the other. We see that she did emulate her to a great extent and wanted to be like her even though she was very much aware of her own station in life and that this could never be. We see that she determined therefore that the way she would be able to experience something similar to that which the one presently referred to as RJ had would be to learn from her and that is exactly what she did. We see that then the one presently referred to as Kathleen would bring this back to the remainder of the women and we see that there would be times when she would be accurate in conveying information and other times not so much. She had a very vivid imagination and would embellish what she had heard or seen.

"There have also been times when we'll be together in a group, Kathleen will come off with something and I'll just go 'I can't believe she said that, it's an outright lie' but I won't say anything. Then when it's the two of us I'll ask her why she lied like that and she'll say, 'You know I did get a little carried away.' This is the same as in that past life."

We see that the one presently referred to as Sue was somewhat aware of this. We see that these two were sisters during that time period and we see that the one presently referred to as Sue was much more practically minded, was much more direct in discerning truth, in judging people and we see that she was very accurate with this. We see that she functioned almost as the group's counselor. She was a kind of connecting link emotionally with the others within the group. We see that she knew that the one presently referred to as Kathleen would embellish stories, but knew that even though she was often affecting that she was also very vulnerable and therefore the one presently referred to as Sue would not embarrass the one of Kathleen in front of the others. There were many encounters between them separately and alone where the one presently referred to as Sue would berate the one of Kathleen for the lies and the one of Kathleen would admit this.

"In this lifetime Kathleen will have feelings about my mother or somebody else but she will talk to me about them. Usually when she's talking to me about it I'm encouraging her to go to that individual and talk directly with them about what she is feeling. She'll go to great extremes not to hurt anybody's feelings. There was one time right after this reading when I was on the phone with her and she went off on something with one of these 'Steel

Magnolias' and I just said, 'Kathleen you know you can say that to me but you don't have the guts to say it to them.' The way I said it was so piercing, I caught myself hurting her. I said to myself, 'Don't go at this, avoid going at this like an ice pick on ice.' I was sharp with it. So I decided my approach would soften with her and be more understanding about where she's coming from."

We see the one presented referred to as Helen was most artistic and creative. She was somewhat flighty in regards to how she would respond to people and situations. She was not very reliable or dependable, but she was very creative and we see that the others did depend upon her in some ways for this kind of creativity for when she could be disciplined in the creativity or when ones of the other women would receive the ideas that she had and would act upon them they were met with great reception by those that these ones served. Therefore, we see that slowly the one referred to as Helen was integrated and accepted more and more into this group as they became more of a cohesive effort. We see that initially upon being brought together they functioned fairly independently, even the two sisters. And we see that they did their jobs well. And we see that there were some hardships that they did face because of this. They had high standards and at times would fall short of them and then would be punished in some way.

"My Aunt Helen had a beauty shop when I got into beauty school so her life and work at that time stimulated my life as a hairdresser today. She has had a shop, and she's in her 70's and it's still going strong. She has almost like a little mecca of a city in Pasadena. It's like Helen's world. Her daughter, RJ, was in business with her. Helen and RJ and my sister Kathleen were all in business together at one point. My mother helped them to buy the real estate for their business. That's Helen's creative part of drawing people together to make something. Her flighty part: Helen has some kind of a value that says happiness is what you own. Happiness is how nice your house is. If your fingernails look right. If your hair looks right."

We see that they worked together and as they began to know one another they began to draw upon each other's strengths. And we see that they created almost what would in present day be referred to as a kind of assembly line where each one exhibited their talents and abilities in particular areas and would work together to come out with a complete product. In this case it would be the dressings. We see that each was substantial in what they offered and they became better and better at what they did.

The one presently referred to as Margorie, we see that that one tended to be a kind of mother for the remaining women. This was even so with the one presently referred to as RJ in time. We see that she was highly protective. She was much more aware of what happened outside of their chosen activities or given activities than any of the other women including the one of RJ even though she lived in that world.

The one presently referred to as Margorie was in contact with some of the males that were in the household and we see that she did often trade sexual favors with them for perks or privileges. We see that she would bring these back to the remainder of the women and share them. We see that it ensured that there was a kind of protection of these women which was not always common within this time and place. We see that she saw this as something that she could offer them and could also protect their chastity by placing her own and using it in the way that she did.

"That is my mother and in a way that's true for today. Today she is married to a judge and a lawyer. And the funny thing is that Margorie has always pretty much worked and not relied on her husband for her money even though she is in a position where she does not have to work. Her husband wants to take care of her. He wants her to quit working and retire with him and travel. But she has a real hard time with that. She has to have money. She has to make her own money. She fears giving it up."

We see that she actually did very little of the work. She was more of what could be considered a consultant. Her major part of the group was the protection that has been described. We see that she was highly insightful however and she did know, she did have knowledge of what would be pleasing to the women that these ones were trying to serve. And we see that this knowledge was passed on and therefore favor was most often given to this group.

"I think my mother has an ability to overlook what is not important. If somebody has something that is really bothering them, she has the ability to look at the whole picture and put it into perspective. She has the ability to focus. I think because of the therapy she has been in, she looks at what directly affects you. If it directly affects you, okay, if it does not directly affect you then don't worry about it. And in some ways that's very good."

The one of Margorie was also insightful in terms of innovations and we see that it was the one presently referred to as Sue that would be able to visualize and conceptualize these ideas and bring them into being. We see that in this way each one contributed something totally unique to the group. We see that the one of Kathleen did contribute the knowledge and perspective of the ones that these ones directly served. We see that she was also a very good worker.

We see for the one of Margorie to have contributed the insight of a kind of expanded vision or worldliness in terms of their place within a greater macrocosm. We see that the one presently referred to as Helen was the creative one in putting together different substances and putting together different types of materials to affect certain looks. The one presently referred to as Sue was the one who was more practically minded who would be able to visualize and conceptualize the ideas and guide the manifestation of them. The one presently referred to as RJ was a kind of motivating factor for these ones for through the contact with her they did derive a great sense of appreciation and love for what they were doing as well as a kind of excitement that was produced from the feedback that they would obtain through her of the work that they had done.

"Visualizing and conceptualizing ideas is a natural for me and my mother is insightful with business. I can see how with what is already in motion, like what the others are doing with a quilt show, I can see how to take what they are already doing and make more money at it. For instance, how you can tie in quilts with stained glass pieces. I can see how to do more with what you are doing whereas in the past lifetime my ideas were directed so we could stay alive. Margorie is probably more insightful. She is in real estate and all of us own real estate. She has been working with Helen to sell her property. She's worked with RJ in selling her property here in Texas, and I bought my house from her. Kathleen has bought property from her. Right now she and Kathleen work together in real estate."

The women were totally separate from those whom they served. It was very rare that they would have any kind of contact with those ones. The major contact was through the one presently referred to as RJ or through stories that the one presently referred to as Margorie would convey. Therefore, because they functioned as a group there was the ability for a much more expanded vision upon their part to be able to have evidence of how they had impacted other people's lives, whether their work was appreciated or not, whether it was acceptable or not as well as how it could be made better.

We see that there were times of squabbles or jealousies that would occur between them and there were even times when they would not speak with one another, but it never did affect the work itself. They continued to work no matter what was occurring between them or what difficulties they might find. We see that there was a very strong sense of connectedness and purpose that they shared that was revolving around their work that did hold them together and that really did take precedence over anything else that might occur. As a result there was much produced and there was much strength that was gained in each of them as individuals.

"My perspective of the Gentle women is the southern belle, and how the southern belle works is that you make your living off the good graces of men. So if you do something that displeases a man, one of the other women will cover for you. So that's where this bond 'no matter what' would come in."

We see that their lives ended when the area was conquered. We see that the place where they stayed was bombarded, it was attacked, and we see that these ones were killed in that. We see that they were forewarned by the one presently referred to as Margorie for she was the one that had the knowledge of what was occurring outside of their realm. And we see that she did encourage the women to take their own life by eating certain plants which were known to be poisonous. We see that this was done as almost a kind of ritual where these ones did take their own life rather than give their life at the mercy of invaders.

"After my refusal to service RJ, she wrote me this letter saying she 'thought that the bond between us was even greater than the men in our lives.' Think about that for a second 'greater than then the men in our lives.' In that past life we all took poison, ate herbs to kill ourselves, so the men in our lives couldn't harm us. What RJ wrote in that letter just flashed in my mind when I was listening to the reading."

The one of RJ was not included in this and did find the bodies and was devastated by it. She lost control of herself mentally and emotionally becoming severely unbalanced. We see that when the attack did occur there were men who took advantage of her before killing her. We see that there was actually very little awareness that she had of what was occurring to her physical body because of the distraught mental and emotional state.

We see for the one presently referred to as Margorie to have withdrawn at the age of 47. She was referred to as Alicina. We see for the one presently referred to as Helen to have withdrawn at the age of 44. We see for her to have been referred to as Sikera. We see for the one of Kathleen to have withdrawn at the age of 39. We see for her to have been referred to as Belatina. We see for the one presently referred to as Sue to have withdrawn at the age of 41. We see for this one to have been referred to as Cacasien. We see for the one presently referred to as RJ to have withdrawn at the age of 40. We see for her to have been referred to as Zula. We see for this time period to be 2370 B.C. This is all.

What was the relationship between the one of Sue and the one of RJ in that past lifetime? Did they have direct contact and what was their degree of relationship?

We see that there were direct contacts between the one presently referred to as RJ and all of the women at one time or another. We see for the one presently referred to as Sue to have been most practically minded as has been stated. We see that she was highly discerning with the one of RJ. We see that the one of RJ at first did not know how to receive this for we see that the one presently referred to as Sue was very direct in the communication and the other one was not used to this. We see however that as the women's relationships evolved that there was more of an intrigue that the one of RJ held for the one of Sue, and the one of RJ began to realize that there were ways that she wanted to be like the one of Sue and therefore she would seek to spend more time in her presence.

We see that it was a very close relationship although it was not necessarily verbal. We see that when the one of RJ was in trouble in terms of an unwanted pregnancy it was the one presently referred to as Sue that she came to. And, as was the role which the one presently referred to as Sue assumed with all the women of being that kind of advisor or counselor, she became this also with the one presently referred to as RJ.

What religion did these follow, if any?

They were not exposed to religion, but they did have a kind of belief that was in a hierarchy of deities or supernatural beings. Much of it was revolving around a kind of predestination or fate.

Very well. What would be the significance of that lifetime to the present lifetime for these five entities?

We see once again for these ones to impact one another in a continually deepening sense. We see that there is a kind of recognition upon their parts of a solidarity, and kind of common bond between them that tends to pervade everything they do and tends to be with them at all times. We see that this does tend to overshadow anything else that will occur. We see that there are times where there will be communication between them and there are times when the communication will break down, but it does not affect this underlying sense of commonality and of pulling together.

We see that there could be much benefit derived by these ones communicating concerning this for it is very elusive to them at the present time period. And we see that there could be much gained through being able to identify what this core contact or communication is concerning.

"No matter what, we all love each other. I know that there were some things that came up with me and I needed help or support, mental and emotional. When it comes to any kind of pain, we are there for each other regardless of the nitpicky stuff. So I think that in our hearts we really love each other and it's deep love. Whatever that bond is, it is directly from the heart and I believe that it is common with all of us. We all love each other."

We see that they each have unique talents and skills once again that are comparable to those described in the previous lifetime and we see that there are ways in which they do impact one another with these. We see that it is not necessarily in regards to the same physical activity as it was in the previous lifetime given, but we see in the present it is more in terms of how they affect one another's psyche or their opinion of themselves, their opinion of the world, their opinion of Creation.

We see that there is a need upon the part of the one presently referred to as Sue for there to be more openness and a greater use of this one's discernment. We see that there is much Truth that this one does perceive, but this one does not always share it. There is a need for this one to adjust this so that this one can be giving and more open in communication with the others.

For the one presently referred to as Helen once again this one is creative, but this one can be somewhat scattered in regards to the thinking. And there is a need for this one to become more direct and purposeful in the use of her creativity. It does not necessitate that this one give up anything which is a fallacy that this one entertains in the thinking. This one needs to learn to be disciplined in order to create what she wants when she wants it. We see that this would be freedom to enjoy life even more.

For the one of Margorie we see that once again there are very definite protective attitudes that this one has and this one will go to extreme lengths to ensure security for herself and those that this one loves. We see that this is an admirable quality, but this one needs to recognize that she need not compromise herself in order to ensure it, that the security that is being sought is inward rather than a change in external security.

"All of us did not like my mother's second husband. He made sexual advances toward me and toward RJ. If we'd taken him up on it he probably would have run fast. But we didn't like him. I loved my stepfather. I loved him a lot, but I didn't like him. I was glad when he died because it freed my mother up so much. She was able to get on with her life. I was never secretive with my mother about how I felt about her second husband. I told her about his sexual advances. In fact, she told me I needed psychiatric help if I had to go to that extreme to get attention from her. But that all worked itself out and there was validity found in it and my stories were backed up by my younger brother. She went directly to each person and we got through it. She quit idolizing her husband and started seeing him for who he was. And she never asked me again if I missed him as much as she did."

We see for the one presently referred to as RJ that there is a need for a recognition of the kind of fullness with which this one is curious about life. This one is once again highly inquisitive and we see that this one does reach to identify the entity, the soul of others rather than be distracted by physical differences or idiosyncrasies. And we see that this is this one's strength. We see that this one often battles within the self in regards to this or feeling put down because of it, and there is a need for this one to come to terms with this and change this way of thinking in order for this one to be able to become the individual that this one is capable of.

"I can see with RJ, I feel like the pain that she had in that past life when she came in and saw all of us dead, I believe it did impact her. And I believe that's part of the reason she does not live in this area, she is away from us.

"She is the only one who does not live in this vicinity. She lives in North Carolina. But you see this way she's not going to have to come down the hill and necessarily see everybody dead which is what happened in that past life. Yet in some ways she's figuratively killed me off because she hasn't really spoken to me since I refused to bring my truck to her aid.

"Another thing, in that past life it said I was very direct and RJ was around me because she wanted to learn that directness. That was very true in this life. When we were teenagers we would go out dancing. Men would come up to our table and RJ could never tell the nerds to go away. RJ would be nice to everybody and I would be the one to say, 'Could you leave the table now please.' And RJ would be like 'Oh thank you'."

For the one of Kathleen we see that there is the desire to be something different than what she is and we see that this one needs to recognize the only limitations to this are those that this one places upon the self. There are no limitations in terms of station in life as existed in the past and we see that to imagine such limitations is to excuse the self from utilizing will power and imagination.

We see that because of these unique differences between them that there is much they have to offer. We see that the strength of one is the weakness of another and we see that by more communication, more investigation, more inquisitiveness with each other in terms of who they are and how they do what they do there could be a great wealth of information born within this group of people. We see that there could be some benefit derived from some type of shared endeavor. This would not necessarily need to be work as it was in the past lifetime, but that there could be any sort of their liking or creation. This would afford them an opportunity to see each other at their best and it would in that way stimulate one another in terms of a greater wholeness within themselves. This is all.

In the present time period these five women are all related. The one of Sue says that although there is a bond of sorts, it seems as if the men in these women's lives are somehow interacted where they seem to impact on the bond to break it apart or interfere with it or the women perceive this in this way, that there is a conflict here. You will examine and relate and offer suggestions concerning this.

We see that within the past lifetime related that this was really not a factor because three of the women were not involved with men at all. The fourth one, the one presently referred to as Margorie was not involved with any one man, but would have short term communications or relations with men that never did affect the group. And the one presently referred to as RJ was not married and the only male that influenced her primarily was her father, also her brothers to a lesser extent than her father. Therefore they did not need to deal with the issue of other relationships. In the present lifetime however these ones have chosen other relationships with the opposite sex of one sort or another. We see that this is an additional factor added into their association.

We see that in actuality the males within the present time period that are close to these females impact the association between the females as much as the females allow it to occur. This is to say that, yes there are unnecessary breakdowns in communication or interferences in their communication that are brought into the relationships by the women themselves. It is not that the men are trying to impose themselves. Once this is understood then there can be a separating of themselves individually and collectively from the other experiences in their lives that involve other people or the men within their lives that they are close to. We see that this is some of the learning that can transpire.

"To understand what the reading is illustrating about the men and these Gentle women, RJ was dating a man from New York, a Jewish man who was married. He took very good care of her. He bought everybody jewelry.

He would just give. And he bought her a townhouse. He moved this huge building onto Helen's property. He did a lot for her money-wise. And when he would come into town, RJ would have her younger lover who lived with her, move out. Then this man, this older married Jewish man, would come be with her and when he left, her younger lover would move back in. And of course we all lived a lie with her."

> *We see that upon the part of some of the men that are attached to these particular women there are conflicts that arise within their individual relationships with the women. We see that there is some jealousy, there is some hostility even, and we see that in the past lifetime related these ones did escape this kind of situation. Not the least of which was the suicides so they would not need to bear their being taken over by aggressive men.*

> *We see in the present time period however these ones are not escaping and they are attempting to have what they consider to be full lives. We see that in including men in their life, there are some individual difficulties that they have in regards to how to be whole within themselves and respond to the people in their lives. We see that in an individual sense this is their independent difficulties that they have in that regard, but in a collective sense there is a kind of fear that the women share that they will in some way lose something should there be openness with the men in their life that they share between themselves. This creates inadvertently a kind of secrecy and a kind of "only we can understand" predominate attitude within the women that is highly irritating to most of the men in their lives and we see that in this way these ones breed a kind of hostility or anger or hurt or jealousy in the men that are involved in their lives. This is unnecessary.*

"My mother had the marriages I've already talked about. My sister in her marriage had an affair with her husband's best friend. Christmas at my aunt Helen's house was real laid back. But when RJ brought a particular man home with her, Christmas at their house totally changed. It was like they had been straight all their life. It was just a totally different family setting and everybody followed along. I didn't understand why all of the sudden this complete personality change except RJ was a princess and everybody served her.

"I think the part I played in all of this was 'Why are we doing this?'

My husband was the one who brought the tendency for pretense to my attention. He said, 'Do you realize that the only time you see RJ is when there is something she needs.' He brought to my attention that in a lot of ways I wasn't getting what I really wanted out of the relationship but I would get whatever I should out of it. When I said no to the tools and the truck, RJ wouldn't accept that it was coming from me, that I had a mind of my own. Of course it was Bob telling me what to do. I think the men in the family would probably get put out with the women just because of how they were in cahoots with each other. There would be importance on one or the other that was out of proportion. Then on the unconscious level realizing that the women were in cahoots with the men."

We see there needs to be a recognition of the differences between the males and the females, a greater awareness of being human, of being people. For when this transition is made there would not be the hostilities that have arisen, there would not be the breakdown in communication, there would not be the unnecessary rifts between the women that tend to be brought into their association because of their reactions to the men. This is all.

Would there be any further suggestions in general for any of these entities, both as a group and for their individual soul growth and development.

We see that within the past lifetime related, all of the time these ones were together except for the one presently referred to as RJ therefore they became very comfortable and accustomed to one another. This is not the case in the present. And we see that there is some difficulty with different members but the more that is being sought is more physicality, more tangible connection rather than an appreciation of their intuitive connection and the development of this. The association itself does lend itself to intuitiveness and to telepathic communication were these ones to accept the validity of such and begin to experiment with it, to cultivate it, to build it. They many times are very much emotionally attuned to one another and can even take on the emotions of one another whether productive or nonproductive. And these are areas which can be explored in the present because of their association. Would suggest that these be developed. (7-26-93-1-BGC)

"RJ has really not talked to me since the time that I didn't drive across town with the truck and the tools. Even though I've called her, I can tell she doesn't want anything to do with me. The last time that I saw her was at a family gathering and I took my stained glass work to this gathering and showed it. In my mind I'm going, "You know you could do quilt designs of this." She and Helen both do quilt shows and it would be very simple to coordinate one of their quilts and do a piece of stained glass that goes with it. Now does this sound like it is connected to that past life? And RJ looked at me and she said, "You stick with the hard stuff, I'll stick with the soft stuff."

"My sister Kathleen never listened to the tape but she did read some of the transcript. She got most of her information from conversations. I have spoken with her about the reading and she has listened. There have been times that things would come up like her embellishing information or my being aware of her inaccuracy with information between myself and RJ or myself and Helen. I was aware of her doing that and I called her on it. I said Kathleen this is what you did in the past and you are doing it right now. And you don't need to do it. Kathleen seemed much more receptive just as in the past life she's the one who is described as wanting to learn.

"This was not the first time my sister had a reading. In another past life reading she was not portrayed very nicely and she was okay with that. Where a lot of people might go, "That's not me!" Kathleen was like, "You know that is kind of like me." Kathleen is just more open than anyone else about the information on the reading. I don't know what changes she has made since the reading except she has been more open with me and my thinking.

"I believe that my cousin RJ was always very curious about the past lives but her mother Helen and I hadn't talked much about it. We were on a low level relationship, we were kind of ebbing at the time of the reading.

"My mother thinks that it's all poppycock. It's like, 'You know, I don't really even want to think about God, okay? I don't want to think about how the universe works. I don't really want to have to think about karma. I don't want to really think about whether I'm gonna go to heaven or hell. I really don't want to do that right now, Sue'."

For Sue's part she has derived much understanding from the reading, about the women in her family and herself. "I think part of my holding back that it refers to in the significance comes from reaching a point where I held back because of the way I would come at them. I used to be almost dogmatic in my beliefs, which was a sign that I really didn't believe. The more people I could get to believe what I believed was helping me to believe what I believed. But then the more I had direct experience and knowledge with something the less I had to do that. So in some ways I back off with them until I can feel common ground and come to them with information that is given in a way that it is received. I believe at the time of the reading there was an evaluation going on. I can see even now where I can do even more of that. Be more open with the truths I know. It's still kind of hard even now.

"These women, I don't like them. I love them but I don't like them. They are constantly in my dreams. So for me they are aspects that I have not completely accepted into my own self. There is a part of them that I didn't like which is a reflection of my own self that I have yet to find harmony with. And so I'm totally blind to a lot of that. I'll have RJ and Helen and Kathleen in my dream and I'm like, 'What happened!' I don't want to see it. So I investigate it and say what about my aunt's uppityness and my cousin's aloofness and my sister's inability to really express herself. I look at our similarities in terms of how can I develop further and it is really hard for me. At this point I'm developing a closer relationship with my aunt and with RJ's daughter and my sister. I'm getting more involved with my mom.

"The reading has also made me aware of the fact that I have that ability to perceive and feel the emotions of another. That was my real connection in the past life with everybody. I believe that in this lifetime I still have a huge emotional connection with all of them. I can feel what RJ feels. I can pick up the phone and she's right there. I can feel Helen. I can feel my mom. I can feel each person and pick up the phone and verify it. All of us have the ability of knowing the other one is going to call or is thinking about the other. I have no doubt in my mind right now that Helen and RJ are probably talking about me.

"The reading says, *'there are times when you are very much emotionally attuned to one another and can take on the emotions of one another whether productive or unproductive.'* That's one thing that I learned from this reading. To be able to separate what my emotions are from theirs because when all of this stuff with my cousin was going down

I was feeling bad and I had to ask myself why. When I could get into *why* I was feeling bad, then I could also decipher that was how RJ was feeling and it wasn't mine."

Over more than ten years, Sue has received many readings from the School of Metaphysics. And she has been instrumental in letting others know about this valuable service. Her repeated contact with this kind of information, both personally and as an interested friend to others getting readings, has aided her to develop the keen insight she displays here in her commentaries. For anyone receiving a reading she suggests the following.

"The first thing I would recommend is to get the reading for yourself. Let that be your first intention. Do it for your own personal understanding, as opposed to doing it for a group. Don't get a reading just to share it with everybody or in hopes that other people will change because of it. Don't think you can really make a difference in the group by everybody getting the reading and everybody joining in and sharing because chances are it won't happen. Go into it with the attitude that what is revealed in the reading is for your own personal learning, your own personal understanding. You are definitely going to grow if that is what your intention is. From there you can share it. You will feel like it is an added bonus when another individual in the family takes the information and goes with it, saying 'I want to know more of this.'

"I have had many different types of readings since the early 1980's and what I have found is that usually, initially, the reading has not been accepted by the family. But as time has passed, like with the first Family Reading I had, each family member in one way or another has come back to me and said 'Remember that reading? What did it say?' My brother has become very interested. He has requested copies of tapes of two Family Readings because he wants to have greater understanding of them.

"For anyone requesting a reading, you will feel delighted when a family member wants more information. Definitely ask their permission and have the reading done and share it with them. Give them copies and transcribe it."

The family structure is unique to mankind. No other animal displays the breadth of choice or the depth of compassion man is capable of. Spouse, father, mother, sibling, aunt, uncle, cousin, grandparent, child, each affords its bearer opportunities for learning and self expression that are very much unique to that role. All afford us opportunities to give and receive love, and together they give us a well-rounded familiarity with this greatest of gifts.

Each time we grow in our understanding of ourselves as spouse or parent or child we expand our soul. Family Readings offer a glimpse of those souls who share our triumphs and defeats, our longings and fulfillments, our desires and fears. They help us understand what motivates the family, individually and collectively. They offer knowledge that fosters communication and enriches the quality of our lives. They tell us what we have that we can give to our family and what family members possess that we might receive.

Above all else, family offers a place to love completely, without reservation. When we are filled with this love we joyously pursue the work of our soul. And that work does indeed become a labor of love.

More About Our Readings

How the Readings Came to Be

The very nature of these readings lends itself to questions. Why is such knowledge so rare? If we have lived before, why can't everyone remember their past lives? Uncovering proof of previous life existences indirectly occurred as a result of the School of Metaphysics' research into mankind's potential and the development of consciousness.

Through years of concentration and meditation practices, individuals have reached deeper and deeper states of consciousness. Lucid dreaming, psi development, intuitive skills, and accumulated wisdom are experienced within these inner levels of awareness. So is memory that extends beyond the boundaries of physical time and reaches into Man's history, collectively and individually. Drawing upon physical memory stored in the brain recalls people, places, and events experienced in the present lifetime. Drawing upon meta-physical memory stored by the soul recalls people, places, and events experienced in previous lifetimes.

The readings currently available through the School of Metaphysics are the result of years of experimentation in the use of the inner mind to produce insights into past lifetime existences and states of health. An effort to use the inner levels to procure knowledge concerning past lives for people other than the person reporting the information eventually led to the first type of reading, the Past Life Reading. Accessing this information had been so helpful for students it was believed that being able to make such knowledge available to anyone would without question aid in their spiritual unfoldment.

The process for reading the past life was repeatedly tested and verified whenever possible. Over several years understanding grew of the process required to garner the information and controls were established to insure the accuracy of what was being perceived and related during a reading. Although future probabilities were discovered to be information available while functioning in the inner mind, delving into the future was determined not to be in alignment with the ideal of the School. By instructing Readers to relate information significant to the present lifetime, profound insights for an individual's growth and soul progression were revealed. This eventually became the Past Life Readings and then the Past Life Crossings. These types of readings continue to relate the information that is most significant, and therefore immediately useable, to the individual(s) requesting the reading.

What people tell us.....concerning Past Life Readings...

"I would like to express my profound thanks to you for the Past Life Reading I have just received. The insight and advice you have given me regarding my way of life are most valuable and highly appreciated. I shall certainly act on them." --- Kevin Lees, Terang, Vic, Australia

"Just wanted to give you some feedback on the past life reading I received from you. The life described is almost a duplicate of my present one! I have as hobbies all the things I was taught in that life. I can sew and embroider darn near anything! Also, I studied painting privately for 18 years and music (piano & organ) for nine years. The desire to be a music composer in that life also makes sense. Although I am not involved in a musical career there are many things about music (for which I have a passion!) that I simply 'know'. I frequently find myself rearranging melodies I hear on the radio to make them more beautiful!

Also I once again chose marriage and family over a career because it was 'expected' of me...In this life I am of Italian descent and marriage and family are very important to us --I have though now taken steps to fulfill some of those unresolved desires. I have not the time to go into how relevant the instructions given to not blame others and trust the creative powers of my inner mind were. In fact, that section of the tape reduced me to tears!

I do hope that sometime next year I will be able to pursue studies with your school..." --Dorothy McDermott, Belle Mead, New Jersey

"I have been a student of Edgar Cayce's readings for some years and always thought how incredibly helpful it would be to find and follow one's true path if there were more 'Cayces' on this planet today, to continue to help lift the veil that hands between ourselves and this greater wisdom. Thank you for the work that you in SOM are doing. This world is in such need for the vision and selfless service that you all provide." -- Gert Basson, Santa Monica, California

"I recently had a past life crossing done and it was quite a remarkable experience. My friend and I wondered about the outcome, but when we heard the reading we were hardly surprised at the nature of the relationship it portrayed. For me it made such complete sense and gave me a sense of incredible calm. Hernan was amazed at the similarities not only between he and I then and now but because the woman your reader described as me, the mother of Hernan, and all the circumstances involving conception, birth, health, life, etc. are identical to his mother now."   -- Patricia Korval, Brooklyn, New York

"Several years ago someone with your organization did a reading regarding a past life crossing with an individual. The reading was hard to believe immediately but over time proved to be remarkably accurate. I wonder if you could do another past life crossing for me with another individual."

-- Marta Been, Boulder, Colorado

more on page 198

Many people find these readings reminiscent of Edgar Cayce's work, a Midwesterner who found he possessed a very real psychic ability which was shared with several hundred people during the early part of the 1900's. It is not chance that during the final quarter of this century, again out of the Midwestern United States, comes a very real psychic ability which has been refined into a skill that can be honed and developed by not just one person, but many. This is in fact the mission of the School of Metaphysics – to respond to what up to this point in history has been in the hands of only a few, revealing what has been kept secret throughout the ages, taught only by small groups ranging from the Freemasons to the Vatican to the Tibetan Buddhist monks and to make that Enlightenment available to anyone who is willing to follow the spiritual disciplines offered.

In addition to the Past Life Readings, the School also offers a Health Analysis. This reading examines the health aura of the individual, relating any mental, emotional, or physical disorder and offering suggestions in each area for wellness and wholeness. The Health Analysis was perfected over several years. From early descriptions relating only the state of the physical body, research expanded to include the emotional influences and eventually the mental causes for physical disorders. In time, the understanding of the specific place in mind to direct the Reader for the attitudinal origin of disorders was discovered and the structure of the Health Analysis was created. Since that time thousands of analyses have been conducted for people to insure good health, as a preventive measure, as a second opinion, and even as a last resort when other health alternatives have failed to identify a problem. The Health Analysis is the subject of another book published by the School of Metaphysics which is widely available.

The discovery that readings could be done without the individual being present was made around 1970 when someone who wanted a Past Life Reading intended to be present but found he could not. This opened the door for people anywhere in the world to receive readings. The first readings from outside the United States were for servicemen stationed in the Phillipines. Since then readings have been done for people all over the world.

As is true with all of the readings, the other types of readings currently offered through SOM were originally designed in response to individuals' requests for assistance. The Business Analysis was in response to a Kansas City businessman who was familiar with the readings offered to individuals and wanted to know more about his business. The Health Analysis structure lent itself well to examining a body, in this case the business vehicle, and its intelligent director, the owner and employees using that vehicle. A book following business owners who have received several Business Analyses over time is currently being researched and we are seeking a benefactor to fund its publication. It will not only offer a complete picture of how this kind of analysis can save money and increase profits but it will offer invaluable spiritual instruction to help any company to realize the highest expression of the service

"Since 1978, when I had my first reading, it has never ceased to astound me at the accuracy of your readings.....I have had eight readings done since 1978. When I have something I can't find the answers to, I request a reading. Because of my skepticism, I give no clues to the School - yet, these readings have been so accurate, I've finally come to taking them at face value as a helpful teacher. Thank you very much." -- Janet Walls, Canfield, Ohio

"I have found two brothers that were discovered through Past Life Crossings. It helped me to understand why I felt so close to these guys I barely knew."
-- Ida Smith, Clinton, Mississippi

"I want to tell you how grateful I am to you for the readings you have done for me in the past year. I believe the School of Metaphysics provides one of the greatest services to others that I have ever found...I would like to share at least a few of the ways in which the readings have benefited my life and other's lives too....In the summer I had a crossing reading. I was torn between whether to continue in a relationship I had or to discontinue the relationship. My grief at losing the relationship was immense but if I chose the relationship, my career would suffer. The reading suggested I look at the desires I had formed aside from the relationship and then see if the relationship fit with those desires. This suggestion enabled me to see that my goals and desires did not fit with the relationship. I am a chemistry student and would have had to drop out of chemistry to continue the relationship. Instead, I applied for a "cooperative education" program (like an internship) in St. Louis. The competition for this opportunity to learn on the job in the chemistry lab is intense. Yet, the interview went well and I was offered the position which I accepted! This is just another way the School of Metaphysics has made a difference in my life. I now have professional experience (and) have been well rewarded financially for my efforts." -- Margaret Kick, Springfield, Missouri

"I requested a family reading for myself, my husband, and our three sons. At the time, I felt we were functioning as five individuals, and not as a family unit. Each person was attempting to go his/her own way, and I couldn't seem to pull (us) together...After receiving the family reading I then had a clear picture of the problems and personality conflicts involved. I was able to comprehend what each one of us as an individual is working on in this present lifetime, and what we are dealing with as a family unit...I highly recommend a family reading (for it) provides the necessary information and insights to those seeking growth in the family structure." -- Lorraine Cochran, Tulsa, Oklahoma

"Thank you for the information your organization has sent to me in the form of Family Readings. I have since February 1984 received my first immediate-family reading, my second family reading in October with other members, and another with my present husband's family in December 1991. The information we all obtained has been extremely enlightening... If I can ever be of service to your organization, or to any other person in question of the value of the readings I am happy to do so." -- Terri Pope, Houston, Texas

more on page 200

it wants to provide and accomplish that mission.

In 1980, a woman in Tulsa wanted a reading on her entire family. Through experiments to find the appropriate structure for this type of information, it was discovered that five people in an immediate family usually shared a common past life experience. With six, however, the probabilities started to decline that all members would be in association at another time. Thus the Family Reading was developed.

In the mid 70's, a young man from Jamaica wrote to SOM asking for help in finding his accurate birth time and date. This stimulated research into what became the Time of Birth Readings.

Some of the most common questions revolve around the talent of the Reader. The ability to give readings is a combination of personal evolutionary development and willingness to serve. The evolutionary development becomes apparent as the individual pursues spiritual disciplines including meditation, astral projection, and thought control. The willingness to serve is necessary in order to effectively master the training which will separate the conscious mind and ego from the subconscious mind which will be literally under the direction of the Conductor during the time the information is given. Becoming a Reader requires a spiritually developed dedication to serve others freely with no thought given to personal reward or gratification.

Conducting readings requires extensive spiritual development in command of the inner levels of mind. One of the contributing authors of this book, Dr. Daniel Condron, has conducted readings for more than 15 years. In the following passage, he describes his early experiences in applying his keenly developed abilities toward developing and producing Readers.

"It was a tough job, plotting uncharted territory, no one to ask questions of when I came to a standstill or a brick wall. At each step, reasoning and will power were required. Reincarnation was a subject that made sense to me from the time I began reading and researching the field, so there was no doubt in my mind concerning past lives or the continuity of our existence. It was only a matter of training another to release the conscious waking mind completely, and follow my mental direction into the deep levels of the inner mind. It was in this manner that over a period of one year of intensive effort that the halls of learning, the universal library also called the Akashic Records, were accessed.

From this point forward, reincarnation was not a matter of belief. I did not believe in reincarnation. Rather, I knew in reincarnation. I know reincarnation to be fact through this and other processes.

In later years, the ability to access the deepest levels of subconscious mind was developed after I trained reader after reader. The ability to be mentally in the inner mind in order to perceive the accuracy and validity of the Health Analysis was developed and obtained through work, effort, time, practice, desire,

About the Health Analysis....

"The accuracy of the reading is quite amazing. The insights into my mental and emotional states are challenging and the suggestions for improvement are inspiring. Studying the reading has quickened the desire in me to work on these issues." -- Sheldon Heckman, Christiansted, St. Croix, U.S.V.I.

"The health reading I had done at the end of January '91 was invaluable to me and·you have my deepest gratitude. According to traditional medicine, I was in 'perfect' health. What was wrong with me didn't show up on their tests and I felt total despair. After receiving the reading, I was at last relieved to know what needed fixing..I have been seeing (a specialist) for a year now and am a 'new' person today." -- Linda Ordogh, Westmount, Quebec, Canada

"I just wanted to write and thank you for my recent health reading. I had been very sick and your reading really helped me to work on the problem from both a spiritual and physical vantage point. And it helped greatly to relieve a lot of my fears. I can't thank you enough for providing this wonderful service."
-- Barbara Lewis, Waggaman, Louisiana

"....Then came a period where I started getting dizzy spells, vague aches and pain and headaches, which was a rare event for me. I went to my doctor which then must have charged the insurance company a few thousand dollars for a battery of tests to find the nature of my illness. The doctor had originally stated to me jokingly that I was either dying or that I was under a great amount of stress. Well, all the tests came back negative. So what was wrong with me?

My fellow meteorologist and metaphysical friend advised me to ask the School of Metaphysics for a health reading, which I did. My first reaction to the reading was one of disappointment, since no physical problem could be found here either. It was mentioned however that I should not be subjecting myself to so much strain.

So I stated my disappointment to my friend and he told me that he and his wife had never heard of a reading that was so brief. Then he allowed me to listen to a reading that he had gotten and was it lengthy. It told where he had a designated vertebrae in his lower neck that was misaligned, and he had me feel that spot and indeed it was. After explaining to me how accurate the other comments had been, I reevaluated my reading, finding it to say more than I had originally heard, and decided that indeed here also was a good reading since it reaffirmed what my doctor had surmised after thousands of dollars worth of tests, that I was under a great amount of stress. Since my job had just been abolished with new duties reassigned whole being in the middle of a massive reorganization going on and doing all of this while working 24 hour around the clock rotation shift work, maybe I was stressed out without really knowing it. Yes, now I was impressed.

more on page 202

and will. This understanding on the part of the Conductor insured that readings were coming from the proper place in mind."

The School of Metaphysics offers a training program resulting in certification as a Reader or Conductor for those who qualify. Student-Teachers pursuing the advanced degree in applied metaphysics study may apply to the Board of Directors for training in this specialized area of concentration. Certification follows a two year internship.

Research continues in refining and developing areas to assist others in greater understanding of Self through the service of readings. Currently, research is being conducted in the deepest levels of consciousness. These readings will transcend the soul, going beyond karmic indentures, and revealing the wisdom which wells up from the individual's Spirit. These readings will hopefully enable the recipient to perceive his highest Self, his Atman, his inner Christ consciousness or Buddha consciousness. In this way we hope to accelerate the evolution and Spiritual Enlightenment of everyone on the planet.

To Secure a Reading

For a quarter of a century, the readings offered through the School of Metaphysics have served to inform and enlighten over one hundred thousand people from six continents. No matter where you live, you can secure a reading at any time from the School of Metaphysics by writing to our headquarters on the campus of the College of Metaphysics in Windyville, Missouri 65783. As you have read, we have spent years refining the readings and ask your cooperation in supplying us with the information we require to serve you in the best way. When we have the correct information from you, we can guarantee the accuracy of your reading.

For any reading we need.....

•The complete name as it appears on the birth certificate for all individuals involved in the reading. *For females who have been married*, we need the first and middle name(s) as they appear on the birth certificate and the most recent husband's last name. This applies even if the female never legally accepted or used that husband's name and it also applies in cases where hyphenated last names have been adopted and are currently used.

•The name and complete address of where you will want the cassette tape of your reading sent.

•A phone number where you can be reached in case questions concerning scheduling your reading arise.

•When you have specific questions relative to the kind of reading you are receiving, feel

..Lastly I'll tell you about a lady meteorologist that we worked with. She was impressed about our stories of Health Readings and decided to get one for herself. However, considering herself a scientist, she was skeptical. So she asked for a reading but intentionally neglected to mention her lifelong respiratory problem. She said she didn't want to give you leading information, and that this was to be her 'ace in the hole' to prove your validity. Then when she started reading the information you sent her, she felt tears come into her eyes as the reading zeroed in on this very problem. 'How could you have known about this?' she wondered. I know she was no longer skeptic and she developed a love for metaphysics...."   -- Anthony Loriso, Clinton, Maryland

"I had a very helpful health reading from you last October. The suggestions, most of which I followed, gave me quite a lot of relief. I was surprised at the suggestion to drink 'whole milk', but followed it and found it great for ridding me of phlegm and bowel waste. The 'goals' I needed to seek have led me to school, where I am presently taking pre-requisite courses for nursing school but I am hesitant, I find my heart not in it because I love tending plants which is what I do now for a living. Thus this request for a life reading. I am grateful you are available, and I thank you and God for the help."
                                                    -- Frances Grove, Phoenix, Arizona

"I was more than pleased with the accuracy of the reading. I want to thank you for helping me mentally, emotionally, and physically. The advice (about an itchy eye problem) that was given to me from my reading proved to be very helpful. My eye condition has improved immensely."
                                                    -- Christine McGinty, Las Vegas, Nevada

"...I am prepared to make two general observations about the readings: 1) The approach is holistic, combining psychological, physiological, and spiritual factors in a manner which orients the subject toward increasing his state of well-being rather than merely focusing on disease care. I strongly approve of this approach. 2) The analysis of the spinal condition as given by the reading was consistent with the clinical X-ray findings."
                                                    -- Mark Genero, D.C., Ann Arbor, Michigan

"You recently did a Health Analysis Reading for me that was truly awesome. The depth and value of the information received was superior. It spoke of truths that only my soul could know and I was in awe of the accuracy. The message was so well-spoken as well. I am grateful to you for this service as I feel certain it will aid in bringing in more light to go higher and help me through some of the issue I have been dealing with. I am delighted to help spread the word about your service. Thank you!" -- Sharla Hawkins, Aurora, Colorado

more on page 204

free to list them and the Conductor of the reading will make sure these issues are covered in your reading.

•Please remember that our readings are offered to aid you in understanding your present situations and circumstances which will enhance your soul progression. For this reason, do not ask us to make predictions on issues you have yet to decide upon. Our readings will not interfere with your right and responsibility to make choices in your life.

•In readings involving others (Crossing of Paths and Family Readings), the consent of all parties involved shows consideration for their privacy and respect for the service the Conductor and Reader are offering.

•If you have questions feel free to call us at 417-345-8411. Someone is available at this number from 8 a.m. to 8 p.m. Central Time everyday.

•When you are ready to mail your request, remember to include at least the suggested minimum donation for each reading mailed. One hundred percent of the donations received for this service contribute to the School of Metaphysics educational services [see About the School of Metaphysics]. Readers and Conductors freely give their time to provide this service to others unencumbered by expectations of personal financial gain.

For Health Readings....
•Since Health Readings are scheduled on a first-come, first-served basis for Tuesday evenings, we must have the complete and exact street address of where you will be between 7 and 11 p.m. (CT) on two consecutive Tuesdays. The street address will either be a *number and street name* or a *route and box number,* plus the city and state. Post Office boxes are fine for mailing, but unless you plan to be in that Post Office box during the time of your reading, this will not tell the Reader where to locate you when your reading is done. Our reading schedules are full so in order to secure your reading, when you give us a place where the Reader will find you be sure you are there.

For Business Analyses....
•Business Analyses are given in response to requests from the owner or responsible governing board of the company. Please feel free to call us should you desire consultation on the type and phrasing of questions to ask during your reading. If you want to be present, arrangements can be made by contacting our headquarters. You will receive a typed transcription as well as an audio cassette of the information given.

Time of Birth Readings...
Readers are trained to isolate the exact physical moment in time when the soul entered the physical body. Knowing the exact time of this commitment affords you the advantages of knowing your subconscious mind's intentions and expectations for this lifetime of learning as it is expressed in your astrological makeup.   To obtain a Time of Birth Reading we need your full name, the date of your birth as it appears on your birth certificate, and the exact street address (as described above for Health Readings) of where you were born.

And the Business Analysis..

"I would like to take the time to thank you for the Business Analysis that we had done by the School of Metaphysics. We have implemented many of the suggestions and it has increased our productivity in many ways. The information concerning our employees was very helpful. I do highly recommend this type of reading to other businesses." -- Martha E. Fuqua, Administrator of New Woman Medical Center, Jackson, Mississippi

"Thank you for the recent business reading you did for my company.... Especially helpful to me was the specific relating of choices I could make to cause new excitement and interest for myself in the business. These had to do with expansion and seeking investment money, and were very detailed as to types of employees I could hire, advertising, taking on a partner, and available options for capitalization. This information has been critical to me in setting forth the direction I will take next in my business. I will recommend this type of reading to other business owners and plan to have another one done next year. This is an excellent evaluation to add to an annual review." -- Cindi Rosenberger, President of Executive Relocation Services, Brentwood, Tennessee

From *Business Ethics Magazine...*

"Life these days can be unsettling and sometimes just plain depressing, what with mass bankruptcies, sudden layoffs, and other recession-era woes. But we've heard of a way to inject a shot of fun back into your work: have a psychic reading done on your company--by a psychic trained to pick up capitalist vibrations. You can find one at the School of Metaphysics, a non-profit educational service organization in Windyville, Missouri. With plans one day to become four-year college, the school rungs workshops on visualization and meditation that attract between thirty and fifty students each weekend, and it has been conducting business readings since its inception in 1973. ....

We'll admit it, we were curious. So we go an acquaintance of ours -- Vic, the owner of a small, nine-person, advertising agency -- to volunteer for a reading....A tape of the reading came back within two weeks. Transcripts followed later. The reading was relatively clear and to the point -- with no moans, altered voices, or jargon. Though Vic remained a bit skeptical, he said the reading gave him some insights. 'I knew there were problems in the company but I'd never been able to pinpoint and solve them.'

The psychic [reader] began with her impressions of the emotional state of the company, saying she sensed confusion around the company -- confusion she attributed to Vic's frustration at being unable to run the company as he would like. She also sensed that many people regularly brought their personal problems to work. And she picked up on a lack of communication between Vic and his employee, as well as problems meeting

Often people desire to be present for their readings. This can occur several times a year at School of Metaphysics centers. If you live in a city where a center is located, direct inquiries to your local director concerning the next available schedule times.

If you live in an area where we have yet to establish a center and want to know what you can do to bring a Reader and Conductor to your city, arrangements can be made by writing to our national headquarters. Often readings are given in conjunction with lecture tours or at special conventions or seminars where Readers or Conductors are featured speakers.

It is a privilege to be able to access this information and offer it as a service to you. Learning how past lives can impact your present relationships and situations, how the quality of your thoughts can be transformed to ensure health and wholeness in mind and body, and how you can use your business as a vehicle for personal growth and service to others, accelerates the exploration and development of consciousness for all of humanity. These readings affirm the availability of peace, wholeness, prosperity, and enlightenment for us all. The information gained can be accessed through years of personal study and spiritual disciplines or through consulting a professional, educated and trained to access the information you desire. It is a honor for the School of Metaphysics to offer this kind of service. We look forward to making these services available to you throughout this lifetime and for many lifetimes to come.

---

deadlines. 'There is difficulty in making commitments and meeting them. Work is seen as a job that has to be done by a certain time, and the creative staff resents that. They don't want to be disciplined.'

In a step unusual for a psychic, she ended with some solutions, such as advising Vic to re-focus his goals. Some of the advcie seemed a bit nebulous, as when [the reader] said employees should learn to make their emotions work for them. And somtimes the advice was impractical, as when she advised hiring a counselor to help employees 'develop more self-awareness' -- a suggestion that would surely prove expensive.

We looked for insights specific to Vic's company, and we found some. For example, Vic asked about an artist who, despite good intentions, continually finishes his work late. From this bit of information, [the reader] identified defensiveness, insecurity, and excessive sensitivity in the artist. As anyone who knows him could tell you, she was right. Now how could she divine that? It seemed more than an educated guess, because being late isn't necessarily a function of defensiveness. [The reader] suggested that if Vic decided to keep this artist, he would need to give him more attention. But that might be difficult, she continued, because Vic shares many of the same negative attributes. Bingo--she was right again.

Based on our experience, if you're looking for new awareness of your company's dynamics, a business reading may be a good place to start." [Vol. 5, No. 5, Sept/Oct 1991]

Additional titles available from SOM Publishing include:

The Dreamer's Dictionary
Dr. Barbara Condron   ISBN 0944386-16-4 $15.00

The Universal Language of Mind: The Book of Matthew Interpreted
Dr. Daniel R. Condron   ISBN 0944386-15-6 $13.00

Permanent Healing
Dr. Daniel R. Condron   ISBN 0944386-12-1 $9.95

Dreams of the Soul - The Yogi Sutras of Patanjali
Dr. Daniel R. Condron   ISBN 0944386-11-3 $9.95

Kundalini Rising - Mastering Your Creative Energies
Dr. Barbara Condron   ISBN 0944386-13-X $9.95

Shaping Your Life - The Power of Creative Imagery
Laurel Fuller Clark   ISBN 0944386-14-8 $9.95

Going in Circles - Our Search for a Satisfying Relationship
Dr. Barbara Condron   ISBN 0944386-00-8 $5.95

What Will I Do Tomorrow? Probing Depression
Dr. Barbara Condron   ISBN 0944386-02-4 $4.95

Who Were Those Strangers in My Dream?
Dr. Barbara Condron   ISBN 0944386-08-3 $4.95

Meditation: Answer to Your Prayers
Dr. Jerry L. Rothermel   ISBN 0944386-01-6 $4.95

HuMan, a novel
Dr. Jerry L. Rothermel   ISBN 0944386-05-9 $5.95

Discovering the Kingdom of Heaven
Dr. Gayle B. Matthes   ISBN 0944386-07-5 $5.95

Autobiography of a Skeptic
Frank Farmer   ISBN 0944386-06-7 $7.95

To order write: **School of Metaphysics National Headquarters**
                     HCR 1, Box 15, Windyville, Missouri 65783

Enclose a check or money order payable to SOM with any order. Please include $2.00 for
postage and handling of books, $5 for international orders.
A complete catalogue of all book titles, audio lectures and courses, and videos is available
upon request.

About the School of Metaphysics

We invite you to become a special part of our efforts to aid in enhancing and quickening the process of spiritual growth and mental evolution of the people of the world. The School of Metaphysics, a not-for-profit educational and service organization, has been in existence for more than two decades. During that time, we have taught tens of thousands directly through our course of study in applied metaphysics. We have elevated the awareness of millions through the many services we offer. If you would like to pursue the study of mind and the transformation of Self to a higher level of being and consciousness, you are invited to write to us at the School of Metaphysics National Headquarters in Windyville, Missouri 65783.

The heart of the School of Metaphysics is a three-tiered program of study. Lessons introduce you to the Universal Laws and truths which guide spiritual and physical evolution. Consciousness is explored and developed through mental and spiritual disciplines which enhance your physical life and enrich your soul progression. We teach concentration, visualization (focused imagery), meditation, and control of life force and creative energies. As a student, you will develop an understanding of the purpose of life and your purpose for this lifetime. Study centers are located throughout the Midwestern United States.

Experts in the language of mind, we teach how to remember and understand the inner communication received through dreams. We are the sponsors of the National Dream Hotline, an annual educational service offered the last weekend in April. Study centers are located throughout the Midwestern United States. If there is not a center near you, you can receive the first series of lessons through correspondence with a teacher at our headquarters.

For those desiring spiritual renewal, weekends at our Moon Valley Ranch offer calmness and clarity. Each Spiritual Initiation Session's mentor gives thematic instruction and guidance which enriches the Spirit and changes lives. One weekend may center on transcendent meditation, another on creative, intuitive writing, *another on wholistic health or understanding your dreams. Please feel free to contact us about upcoming sessions.*

The Universal Hour of Peace was initiated by the School of Metaphysics at noon Universal Time (GMT) on October 24, 1995 in conjunction with the 50th anniversary of the United Nations. We believe that peace on earth is an idea whose time has come. To realize this dream, we invite you to join with others throughout the world by dedicating your thoughts and actions to peace for one hour beginning at noon [UT] on the first of January each year.

There is the opportunity to aid in the growth and fulfillment of our work. Donations are accepted and are a valuable way for you to aid humanity by supporting the expansion of the School of Metaphysics' efforts. As a not-for-profit publishing house, SOM Publishing is dedicated to the continuing publication of research findings that promote peace, understanding and good will for all of Mankind. It is dependent upon the kindness and generosity of sponsors to do so. Authors donate their work and receive no royalties. We have many excellent manuscripts waiting for a benefactor.

One hundred percent of all donations made to the School of Metaphysics are used to expand our services. Donations are being received for Project Octagon, the first educational building on the College of Metaphysics campus. The land for the proposed campus is located in the beautiful Ozark Mountains of Missouri, less than four hours from St. Louis and Kansas City, and one hour north of Springfield. The four-story octagon design will enable us to increase headquarters staff and enrollment in our College workstudy program. This proposed multipurpose structure will include an auditorium, classrooms, library and study areas, a cafeteria, and potential living quarters for up to 100 people. Gifts may be named for the donor or be designated as an ongoing memorial fund to a family member or special friend. Donations to the School of Metaphysics are tax-exempt under 501(c)(3) of the Internal Revenue Code. We appreciate any contribution you are free to make. With the help of people like you, our dream of a place where anyone desiring Self awareness can receive wholistic education will become a reality.

We send you our Circle of Love.